D1500317

LEADERSHIP

PRACTICAL AND PROVEN APPROACHES
IN LEADERSHIP AND SUPERVISION

ESSENTIALS

Olin O. Oedekoven, Ph.D.

John Lavrenz, MS

Deborah Robbins, MPA

Oedekoven, O.O., Lavrenz, J., & Robbins, D.K. (2014). **Leadership Essentials: Practical and Proven Approaches in Leadership and Supervision.** Gillette, Wyoming: Peregrine Leadership Institute.

ISBN: 978-0-9908279-0-0 (Hardcover Edition)

ISBN 978-0-9908279-0-0

52995>

9 780990 827900

Revised 2015.

We would like to dedicate this book to John Lavrenz. John was our co-author on the project, colleague and presenter with our leadership development workshops, a mentor to so many leaders over the years, and, most importantly, our friend. His leadership influence is felt throughout in these pages and will continue with all of the lives he touched during his values-based leadership journey. John "walked the talk" as a leader of integrity, and we are all richer for the time we have spent with him.

— Olin O. Oedekoven and Deborah K. Robbins

Table of Contents

Foreword

This is not a book that you have in your hands. A book, after all, is merely a set of written sheets of paper hinged together on one side in a fashion that allows readers to flip through and glance casually at each side.

This is an understanding. It is a collective release of leadership tips and techniques as simple as your most basic needs, yet as complex as the very nature of the cultural diversities in which you live today. It is a manual on how to live in a world where globalization and technological advances have toppled the walls of traditional leadership hierarchies, a world in which leaders must come to know and understand the evolution of change and how to develop, inspire, and guide their organizations [and their careers] through the tactical challenges coming at them both faster and more different than ever before.

This is a way of understanding how to survive in the ever changing world of leadership. It is a compilation of many years of experience, of those lessons we learned along our own leadership journeys. We lived and breathed every minute of this guide, shedding tears of frustration during those tenuous times and emitting guttural episodes of laughter when everything fell into place and we achieved leadership excellence. We held nothing back. When we made the decision to put into words all that we have experienced during our own leadership upbringings, it only made sense to bare it all, to include not only our brief moments of fame, but those often staggering moments of shame as well. After all, "that which does not kill us only makes us stronger." To achieve success in today's highly complex world of leadership, you simply must be open to the fact that change is inevitable and the rate at which we have been changing has grabbed headlines for many years. Nations as a whole are experiencing dramatic shifts in their political, economic, and social structures. Words such as demographics and cultural awareness were once nothing more than mandatory inclusions in company handbooks, policies, and procedures. Now the very essence of those generational and cultural differences is driving decision making like never before One of the key skills of effective leadership is the ability to lead change. Your survival depends on it.

Remember, leaders are made, not born. We made mistakes and so will you. However, your ability to get up, dust yourself off, and set yourself at the front of the pack again and again is what will set you apart from those individuals who only wish they were leaders. We don't profess to know everything there is to know about leadership. What we do know, we've included in this guide. Read it well and return to it often. Each chapter contains real lessons learned from real people. This is your first step down a lifelong journey called leadership. Good luck and let the journey begin.

Chapter 1

Understanding Leadership

Leadership Defined

Leadership is the process of influencing others to understand and agree about what needs to be done, how it can be done effectively, and the process of facilitating individual and collective efforts to accomplish the shared objectives.

Influencing ... getting people to willingly do what you want them to do ... How do leaders influence?

- Communicate (written, verbal, nonverbal)
- Set the example
- Demonstrate what "right looks like"

Understand and Agree ... giving reasons for why we do what we need to do. How do leaders develop understanding and agreement?

- Communicate company goals (bigger picture)
- Our mission/vision
- Our departmental goals

Done Effectively ... The way you want to accomplish what it is that you want to accomplish. How do leaders develop effectiveness?

- Setting and maintaining standards
- Teaching, coaching, and mentoring for performance

Facilitating Individual and Collective Efforts ... Developing interest, will, desire, and ensuring the resources are there for them to do what it is that you need them to do. How do leaders facilitate effort?

- Give employees a challenge
- When they succeed, praise them
- Coach/counsel them on how to do it better
- Set the example through your behaviors and actions
- Provide the resources they need for the mission

Accomplish the Shared Objectives ... the goals, objectives, and the vision. How do leaders develop an understanding of the shared objectives?

- Communicate, Communicate, and Communicate!
- Team planning and preparing
- Assessing after the project is completed

You manage things, you lead people. Management is about doing things right. Leadership is about doing the right things. Leadership depends on the situation, the work setting, and the nature of the problem. Leadership also shifts with time and responsibilities. Leadership and Management are not mutually exclusive activities.

You do not have to have subordinates to be a leader — being a leader means striving to BE, KNOW, and DO what is right, all the time. We will, however, make mistakes. How we deal with those mistakes is what distinguishes us as a learning leader.

The Values and Attributes of Leadership

There are seven essential values and seven critical attributes of leadership.

Leadership Values

Integrity: Demonstrating the personal courage necessary to support your leadership values and the values of the organization; exemplifying your values at all times; treating others fairly and consistently; choosing the harder right over the easier wrong; doing the right things, not just doing things right. This leadership value is essential. If you do not display this value in your behavior at all times, you may not have the opportunity to recover.

Honesty: Being honest in all your communications, interactions with others, and with yourself; saying what you mean and meaning what you say.

Loyalty: Fulfilling your obligations to your team, peers, and superiors; being loyal to your team and your organization with support on and off the job; remaining faithful and steadfast to your values; holding what others say in trust.

Accountability: Being accountable for all your actions and the results of those actions; remembering that while you can delegate authority, you can never delegate responsibility – you, as the leader, are always responsible for the successes and failures of your team, acknowledging the contributions of others, and assuming the responsibility even when others will not.

Respect: Being a leader who treats others with respect; treating others fairly and consistently; giving away respect and not making others have to earn your respect; respecting, acknowledging, and publicly recognizing the contributions of others.

Trust: Being approachable, acknowledging, considerate, accepting, and respectful towards others; building trust within your team through open and honest communications; demonstrating compassion and understanding towards others.

Unselfishness: Being a leader who gives credit where credit is due; helping others with the mundane tasks, making a sincere and honest effort to examine problems and issues from the perspective of others; putting the needs of others before those of your own; promoting the interests of the team and the organization ahead of your own.

Seven Key Leadership Attributes

Self-Discipline: Maintaining self-control over your emotions, temper, and language; following through with what you say you will do; choosing the best course of action that will support the organizational goals; maintaining your enthusiasm and spirit even when the situation is difficult.

Initiative: Seeing what needs to be done and doing it without having to be told what to do; encouraging others to participate and promote their ideas; giving credit where credit is due; conduct both formal and informal assessments for all work that has been completed to help foster continuous improvement in the workplace.

Confidence: Exercising good judgment with people and the work that needs to be done; maintaining your perspective of the bigger picture and the goals of the organization; acting with courage during the difficult times.

Decisive: Making sound, timely decisions and communicating your decisions clearly and concisely; not withholding decisions that you should be making; remaining steadfast with your decisions, but being open to adapting to new information or changed conditions; not yielding to impulses, but rather examining problems logically and systematically without prejudice or bias.

Valuing Diversity: Respecting cultural differences; maintaining cultural awareness; appreciating the value of diversity and the benefits that diversity brings to an organization; being mindful and respectful of differences in the workplace and understanding what it takes to successfully motivate, inspire, and lead the cultural and generational differences that exist within the organization.

Empowering: Enabling others to make decisions on their own by providing them with an understanding of your intent along with any information needed to make good decisions on their own; not micromanaging the work; encouraging others to take the initiative; promoting others' ideas and giving credit where credit is due; recognizing and rewarding the achievement of others.

Humility: Recognizing that it is not about you — it is about the success of your team and the organization; looking outward to attribute success and looking inward to apportion failure; maintaining your sense of humor — always taking the work seriously, but not taking yourself too seriously.

The Power of Positive Expectations[1]

The concept of Pygmalion Leadership has its roots in ancient Greek mythology. It is the general belief that your employees will rise only to the level that you expect them to rise. That is, what you expect of your employees will have a direct bearing on the outcomes. It is your expectations that will drive team performance. If you believe that a person will fail, most likely they will believe it as well (and fail). If, on the other hand, you believe that a person will succeed and the person knows this expectation, most people will rise to the level you expect from them.

The Self-Fulfilling Prophecy

People may have an extraordinary influence on others —
an effect of which they are often not aware. Psychologists
have demonstrated that the power of expectation alone can
influence the behavior of others. The phenomenon has been
called the "self-fulfilling prophecy" or the "Pygmalion effect."
People sometimes become what others expect them to
become. Many supervisors are able to develop competent
employees and stimulate their performance. What is their
secret? How is the successful supervisor different from the
unsuccessful ones, the supervisors who cannot develop their
employees? What are the implications of this for the growing
problem of turnover and disillusionment among promising
employees? The concept of the self-fulfilling prophecy shows
how it can either be a useful or a destructive tool in the
hands of the supervisors.

The Pygmalion Effect

All it takes is really believing. Supervisors can create better
employees by simply believing in them. This is even truer when
working with underachievers.

If you tell a grammar school classroom teacher that a child is
bright, the teacher will be more supportive, teach more difficult
material, allow more time to answer questions, and provide
more feedback to that child. The child receiving this attention
and basking in the teacher's beliefs learns more and is better
in school. It does not matter if the child is actually bright. All
that matters is that the teacher believes in the child. This is
also true of managers and workers.

This uniquely human phenomenon is called the Pygmalion
effect. It is a persistently held belief in another person such
that the belief becomes a reality. The person believed in, the
one being believed, becomes the person whom they are
perceived to be.

Did you ever notice that there are some people with whom we naturally feel comfortable? Those who think our ideas are great. When they listen to us we express ourselves clearly and are able to make ideas ring with clarity and insight. This is because they, believing we are bright, see us in this light. We, in turn, knowing how they feel about us, work hard to make sure they are satisfied with our answers.

The opposite is also true. There are people with whom we are not comfortable and who we believe do not like us. We avoid these people and do not do our best when we are around them. With these people we are hesitant and much less articulate. Most of the time we are less likely to try very hard to be understood. We are victims of a label that has been placed on us by someone else.

This is also true in the supervisor/employee relationship. Researchers looked at 12 separate research studies from different work settings involving a total of 2,874 participants and using a technique called meta-analysis. All studies involved employees and their supervisors (the people who were responsible to oversee and evaluate their work). Each study randomly assigned employees to two groups and supervisors were told that one group of employees had considerably greater potential than the other group. Thus, a positive attitude was fostered on the part of supervisors about one group of employees who were basically no different than the employees in the other group.

Employees in the group for which the supervisors were given positive information responded with greater productivity with only two exceptions. The magnitude of these gains seemed to be dependent on the circumstances of the work relationship. The greatest gains were seen in military training settings. The researchers suspect that this is because in the military it is easier to control the information supervisors receive, whereas, in a business situation, word-of-mouth and reputation may bleed into the situation making the positive information received by the supervisor less believable. However, when looking at findings in elementary school settings, there seems to be something that happens in a learning situation that is different from what happens in a work situation. It is possible that a positive attitude on the part of supervisors may have a greater effect on learning than it does on work productivity.

The second greatest gains were obtained in situations where disadvantaged workers (those who for whatever reason were less likely to be successful) were randomly assigned to two groups. The group, for which the supervisor was given positive information, made significant gains over the group for which the supervisor was not given positive information. It is suspected that people with low self-esteem and self-efficacy are more likely to respond to positive feedback. This indicates that supervisors have the potential to create high performing employees. All that is needed is for them to believe that an employee has potential — the Pygmalion effect. This is probably because the employee is more fully engaged and motivated when working for a positive thinking supervisor, thereby allowing the organization to fully tap into his or her capabilities.

There were fewer gains noted when supervisors had less direct interaction with subordinates, such as in sales situations where employees worked independently and away from their supervisor. In addition, women supervisors were less likely to be affected by the Pygmalion effect. It was observed that women, regardless of their beliefs, seemed to treat employees equally. Therefore, the group of employees about whom a woman supervisor was given positive information made less significant gains over the other group. This was even more pronounced when the supervisor and all the employees were women.

The Pygmalion Effect could be an important key to creating or improving a work force. Everything should be done to create a highly positive attitude about employees in the minds of supervisors, and employees should be made to feel that their supervisors and the organization believe in their potential as people.

Leaders should present new employees to supervisors in a positive light while highlighting the new employee's potential and making sure that the supervisor and the work group have a clear expectation that the new employee will make a significant impact on the work group's ability to succeed. Supervisors should be trained in how to impart a positive motivating attitude that fosters a belief in the employee's ability to perform.

Employees should have a clear understanding that there is no question of them performing well. Employees should be given training opportunities which bring out potential rather than focus on weaknesses. Over all, the organization should strive to create an understanding among its employees that they all have potential and all that is needed is for that potential to be brought out.

Climate

Negative Pygmalion

Poor behaviors that communicate low expectations include:

- Being distracted, in a hurry, or to not give an employee your full attention
- Verbally criticizing their competence or potential
- Negative non-verbal cues through tone of voice, or face and body gestures

Positive Pygmalion

Good behaviors that communicate high expectations include:

- Being verbally supportive and encouraging
- Providing positive non-verbal cues through tone of

voice, eye contact, facial expressions, body posture, and movements

- Helping employees set challenging goals

Input

Negative Pygmalion

Poor behaviors that communicate low expectations include:

- Not giving people vital information to do a job
- Not giving people sufficient direction or guidance
- Waiting too long to check on progress or provide any needed course correction
- Treating people like they are incompetent by providing only limited or sketchy information (only on a "need to know" basis)

Positive Pygmalion

Good behaviors that communicate high expectations include:

- Spending extra time with people
- Providing ideas to follow up on or sources for further information (giving the team enough resources or ideas while allowing them to retain autonomy and ownership of projects)

Output

Negative Pygmalion

Poor behaviors that communicate low expectations include:

- Cutting people off when they are speaking
- Not seeking their opinions or insights
- Limiting the number and scope of their work assignments

Positive Pygmalion

Good behaviors that communicate high expectations include:

- Allowing them to express their opinions and ideas (even disagreeing opinions)
- Giving them new assignments (or a variety of assignments including incrementally challenging assignments)
- Giving them opportunities to learn or practice skills (e.g. training, projects)
- Allowing them to gain exposure to, and visibility with, other people and departments (especially upward in the organization)

Feedback

Negative Pygmalion

Poor behaviors that communicate low expectations include:

- Providing mostly negative, vague, or limited feedback
- Criticizing the person (instead of the behaviors), making negative generalizations (e.g. negative labels)

Positive Pygmalion

Good behaviors that communicate high expectations include:

- Providing helpful suggestions on how people might be able to improve or do things better
- Positively reinforcing desirable behaviors (praise, recognition, rewards, etc.). This should be sincere, specific and frequent enough
- Making sure any feedback regarding poor performance is done in a positive way, wherein the employee can sense that you have their best

interests at heart and you reinforce your belief in their ability to do better

Expectations

A well-defined expectation is the foundation for goal achievement. It formalizes:

- What is to be accomplished
- Who will be involved
- When the activity will be accomplished
- How resources will be used

Expectations should include team values and team rules. Make life easier for yourself — write down the expectations, rules, and your code of conduct, and share these with your team.

S. M. A. R. T. Objectives

Specific
    Measurable
        Achievable
            Realistic
                Time-Bound

In summary, use the Pygmalion Effect, often known as the Power of Expectations, by considering:

- Every supervisor has expectations of the people who report to him/her.
- Supervisors communicate these expectations consciously or unconsciously.
- People consciously or unconsciously pick up on these expectations from their supervisor.
- People perform in ways that are consistent with the expectations they have picked up on from the supervisor.

The Pygmalion Effect enables team members to excel in response to a manager's message that they are capable of success and expected to succeed. The Pygmalion Effect can also undermine staff performance when the subtle communication from the manager tells them the opposite. These cues are often subtle and examples of this include when a supervisor fails to praise a staff person's performance as frequently as he/she praises others or when a supervisor talks less to a particular employee than to others.

Principles for People Development

Success in developing others is how well you accomplish each of the following:

- **Value People:** Concerns attitude
- **Commit to People:** Concerns time
- **Integrity with People:** Concerns character
- **Standard for People:** Concerns vision
- **Influence over People:** Concerns leadership

Successful People Developers are those who:

- **Make** the right assumptions about people
- **Ask** the right questions of people
- **Give** the right assistance to people

What you believe about yourself influences what you believe about your people. We are measured not by what we are, but by the perception of what we seem to be; not by what we say, but how we are heard; and not by what we do, but how we appear to do it.

Positive Pygmalion Characteristics

- Belief in themselves and confidence in what they are doing.

- Belief in their ability to develop the talents of their employees: to select, train, and motivate them.

- Ability to communicate to workers that their expectations are realistic and achievable.

- Belief that workers can learn to make decisions and to take the initiative.

- Preference for the rewards that come from the success and increased skills of their subordinates over the rewards they get from their supervisors.

Everything Rises and Falls on Leadership

- Personnel determine the potential of the organization.

- Relationships determine the morale of the organization.

- Structure determines the size of the organization.

- Vision determines the direction of the organization.

- Leadership determines the success of the organization.

The 14 Characteristics of Great Leaders

Integrity: The qualities of absolute honesty, trustworthiness, uprightness of character, and high moral principles. Integrity can be practiced by doing the following:

- Tell the truth to both superiors and subordinates, all the time.

- Stand for what you believe in, even if the belief is unpopular.

- Use your power to work toward your organization's goals or for the welfare of your co-workers and not for your own personal gain.

Knowledge: You will quickly gain the respect and confidence of your employees by showing them you are knowledgeable about your area of responsibility as well as theirs. Keep in mind that learning is a continual process. To develop and demonstrate knowledge you should:

- Ask questions when unsure.
- Notice and correct substandard performance in others, particularly those who work for you.
- Show your employees, by your actions, how they should perform their duties.

Courage: Courage is the quality that acknowledges fear but allows you to meet danger or opposition calmly and with firmness. Courage is developed when you:

- Place duty and commitment to your organization's mission over personal feelings and desires.
- Look for and willingly accept responsibilities.
- Stand for what is right, even if it is unpopular.
- Never blame others for your mistakes.

Decisiveness: Decisiveness is the ability to weigh all the facts and make timely decisions. To develop decisiveness, you should:

- Get into the habit of considering several points of view for each problem, and then make your best choice.
- Know when not to make a decision.
- Remember that a good decision now is usually better than a perfect decision later.
- Be willing to adjust your decision if you realize it is no longer effective.

Dependability: Leaders are dependable when they fulfil their commitments. Dependability is developed by:

- Being on time and prepared.

- Accomplishing your assigned tasks, even if you face obstacles.

- Building a reputation for keeping your word when you have made a promise.

- Demonstrating loyalty to your friends and supporters.

Initiative: Initiative is recognizing what must be done and then doing it without being told to do so. Practice the following to develop initiative:

- Find tasks that need to be done and then do them without being told.

- Look for better ways to do things.

- Consider strategic issues and look for ways to overcome future obstacles.

Tact: Tact is the ability to deal with others without causing ill feelings or offense. In order to develop tact, do the following:

- Apply the Golden Rule: Treat others as you would want to be treated.

- Check yourself for tolerance and patience. If you lack these qualities, make efforts to change.

Justice: To be just is to be fair. Personal feelings, emotions, and prejudices must not be allowed to influence your decisions. To improve the trait of justice, make sure you practice the following:

- Apply rewards and reprimands to all consistently.

- Listen to all sides of an issue before making a decision.

- Be aware of your counter-productive prejudices and seek to rid yourself of them.

Enthusiasm: Enthusiasm is showing sincere interest and

eagerness in performing your job. To develop enthusiasm in others, you should:

- Consistently exhibit a positive attitude towards others.
- Emphasize the employee's successes.
- Encourage others to overcome any obstacles that they encounter.

Bearing: Your bearing is your general appearance and conduct. Bearing is demonstrated by:

- Controlling your voice and gestures so that emotional extremes do not show in your actions. Sometimes it is appropriate to show some anger, but you should never appear to lose your temper.
- Not reprimanding anyone in the presence of others.

Endurance: Maintaining the physical and mental stamina to perform your job under difficult conditions and for long periods of time. Maintain endurance by doing the following:

- Avoid activities that lower your physical and mental stamina.
- Maintain a proper diet and exercise.
- Finish every job, regardless of the obstacles.

Unselfishness: You should always give credit where credit is due. To be unselfish you should:

- Give credit to employees for jobs well done and ensure that any recognition or praise from higher levels is passed on to deserving individuals.
- You will be surprised at how much respect you will receive from employees when you help them with some of their tasks.
- Make a sincere, honest attempt to look at situations from the other person's perspective.

Loyalty: Loyalty is the quality of faithfulness to your principles, your country, your organization, your superiors, and your subordinates. To practice loyalty you should:

- Remember loyalty is a two-way street. Be loyal to those above and below you.

- Stand up for your organization and its members when they are unjustly attacked.

- Discuss your problems with those who can help solve the problems. Do not gossip.

Judgment: Judgment is the ability to weigh facts logically, to consider possible solutions, and to reach sound decisions. Judgment includes using common sense. To develop the trait of judgment, you:

- Do not yield to impulse. Think about the possible effects of what you are about to do.

- Try to visualize the situation from the other person's perspective. When in doubt, seek good counsel from those who can best help you.

---

1. Adapted from *The Pygmalion Effect: Managing the Power of Positive Expectations, Participant's Workbook. (2001).* Carlsbad, CA : CRM Learning, L.P.

Chapter 2

Teams, Teamwork and Leadership Styles

Leadership Styles

All people are shaped by what they have seen, what they have learned, and whom they have met. Who you are determines the way you work with other people. Some people are happy and smiling all the time. Others are serious. Some leaders can wade into a room full of strangers and within five minutes have everyone engaged and thinking, "How have I lived so long without meeting this person?" Some very competent leaders are uncomfortable in social situations. Most of us are somewhere in between. Although leadership theory describes at great length how you should interact with your subordinates and how you must strive to learn and improve your leadership skills, you must always be yourself. Anything else comes across as fake and insincere.

Effective leaders are flexible enough to adjust their leadership style and techniques to the people they lead and the situations they encounter. Some subordinates respond best to coaxing, suggestions, or gentle prodding. Others need, and sometimes even want, the verbal equivalent of a kick in the pants. Treating people fairly does not mean treating them as if they were clones of one another. In fact, if you treat everyone the same way, you are probably being unfair because different people need different things from you.

Think of it this way. Suppose you must teach safety procedures to a large group of employees ranging in experience from new employees to very experienced employees. The senior employees know a great deal about the subject while the new employees know very little. To meet all their needs, you must teach the new employees more than you teach the senior employees. If you train the new employees only on the advanced skills the senior employees need, the new employees will be lost. If you make the senior employees sit through training on the basic tasks the new employees need, you will waste the senior employee's time. You must match the training (and your leadership) to the experience of those being trained. In the same way, you must adjust your leadership style and techniques to the experience of your people and characteristics of your organization.

Obviously, you would not lead senior team members the same way you would lead new employees. But the easiest distinctions to make are those of rank and experience. You must take into account personalities, self-confidence, self-esteem — all the elements of the complex mix of character traits that make dealing with people so difficult and so rewarding. One of the many things that makes your job tough is that you must figure out what your subordinates need and what they are able to do in order to get their best performance even when they do not know themselves.

When discussing leadership styles, many people focus on the extremes, autocratic and democratic. Autocratic leaders tell people what to do with no explanations. Their message is, "I am the boss. You will do it because I said so." Democratic leaders use their personalities to persuade subordinates. There are many shades in between. The following paragraphs discuss five of them. However, bear in mind that competent leaders mix different elements of all these styles according to place, task, and people involved.

Using different leadership styles in different situations or elements of different styles in the same situation is not inconsistent. Rather, the opposite is true. If you are only able to use one leadership style in a given situation, then you are inflexible and will have difficulty operating in situations where that style does not fit.

Directing Leadership Style

The directing style is leader-centered. Leaders using this style do not solicit input from their respective subordinates. They give detailed instructions on how, when, and where they want a task performed. They then supervise its execution very closely.

The directing style may be appropriate when time is short and leaders do not have a chance to explain things. They may simply give orders: Do this; Go there; Move. Leaders may revert to this style in fast paced operations or in emergency situations, even with experienced subordinates. But if the leader has created a climate of trust, subordinates will assume the leader has switched to the directing style because of the circumstances.

The directing style is also appropriate when leading inexperienced teams or individuals who are not yet trained to operate on their own. In this kind of situation, the leader will probably remain close to the action to make sure things go smoothly.

Some people mistakenly believe the directing style means using abusive and demeaning language, or threatening and intimidating others. This is wrong. If you are ever tempted to act this way, whether due to pressure, stress, or what seems like improper behavior by a subordinate, ask yourself these questions. Would I want to work for someone like me? Would I want my boss to see and hear me treat subordinates this way? Would I want to be treated this way?

Participating Leadership Style

The participating style centers on both the leader and the team. Given a job to do, leaders ask subordinates for input, information, and recommendations, but make the final decision on what to do themselves. This style is especially appropriate for leaders who have time for such consultations or who are dealing with experienced subordinates.

The team-building approach lies behind the participating leadership style. When subordinates help to create a plan it becomes, at least in part, their plan. This ownership creates a strong incentive to invest the effort necessary to make the plan work. Asking for this kind of input is a sign of a leader's strength and self-confidence. But asking for advice does not mean the leader is obligated to follow it. The leader alone is always responsible for the quality of decisions and the outcome of plans.

Delegating Leadership Style

The delegating style involves giving subordinates the authority to solve problems and make decisions without first clearing them through the leader. Leaders with mature and experienced subordinates, or who want to create a learning experience for subordinates, often need only to give them authority to make decisions along with the necessary resources and a clear understanding of the mission's purpose. As always, the leader is ultimately responsible for what does or does not happen, but in the delegating leadership style, the leader holds subordinate leaders accountable for their actions. This is the style most often used by managers dealing with senior supervisors and by organizational and strategic leaders.

Transformational and Transactional Leadership Styles

There is a distinction between the transformational leadership style, which focuses on inspiration and change, and the transactional leadership style, which focuses on rewards and punishments. We do not deny that the rewards and punishments are effective and sometimes necessary. However, carrots and sticks alone do not inspire individuals to excel.

Transformational Leadership Style

As the name suggests, the transformational style "transforms" subordinates by challenging them to rise above their immediate needs and self-interest. The transformational style is developmental. It emphasizes individual growth (both professional and personal) and organizational enhancement. Key features of the transformational style include empowering and mentally stimulating subordinates. The transformational leaders consider and motivate team members as individuals first, and then the group as a whole. To use the transformational style, you must have the courage to communicate your intent and then step back and let your subordinates work. You must also be aware that immediate benefits are often delayed until the job or task is accomplished.

The transformational style allows you to take advantage of the skills and knowledge of experienced subordinates who may have better ideas on how to accomplish a mission. Leaders who use this style communicate reasons for their decisions or actions, and, in the process, build a broader understanding and ability to exercise initiative, and operate effectively with subordinates.

Not all situations lend themselves to the transformational leadership style. The transformational style is most effective during periods that call for change or when presenting new opportunities. It also works well when organizations face a crisis, instability, mediocrity, or disenchantment. It may not be effective when subordinates are inexperienced, when the mission allows little deviation from accepted procedures, or when subordinates are not motivated. Leaders who use only the transformational leadership style limit their ability to influence individuals in these and similar situations.

Transactional Leadership Style

In contrast, some leaders employ only the transactional leadership style. This style includes such techniques as:

- Motivating subordinates to work by offering rewards or threatening punishment.

- Prescribing task assignments in writing.

- Outlining all the conditions necessary to complete the task, including the applicable rules and regulations, the benefits of success, and the consequences to include possible disciplinary actions of failure.

- "Management-by-exception," where leaders focus on their subordinates' failures, showing up only when something goes wrong.

The leader who relies exclusively on the transactional style, rather than combining it with the transformational style, evokes only short-term commitment from subordinates and discourages risk-taking and innovation.

There are situations where the transactional style is acceptable, if not preferred. For example, a leader who wants to emphasize safety could reward the organization, if the organization prevents any serious safety-related incidents over a two-month period. In this case, the leader's intent appears clear. Safe habits are rewarded, but unsafe acts will not be tolerated.

However, using only the transactional style can make the leader's efforts appear self-serving. In this example, employees might interpret the leader's attempt to reward safe practices as an effort to look good by focusing on something that is unimportant but that has the boss's attention. Such perceptions can destroy the trust, subordinates have in the leader. Using the transactional style alone can also deprive subordinates of opportunities to grow, because it leaves no room for honest mistakes.

The most effective leaders combine techniques from the transformational and transactional leadership styles to fit the situation. A strong base of transactional understanding, supplemented by charisma, inspiration, and individualized concern for each subordinate, produces the most enthusiastic and genuine response. Subordinates will be more committed, creative, and innovative. They will also be more likely to take calculated risks to accomplish their mission. Looking back to the safety example we used earlier, leaders can avoid any misunderstanding of their intent by combining transformational techniques with transactional techniques. They can explain why safety is important (intellectual stimulation) while, at the same time, encouraging their subordinates to take care of each other (individualized concern).

Leading Teams

Few leadership roles are as important in empowered organizations as team building. Effective teamwork is the foundation of productivity. In this chapter we will explore several important topics concerning team leadership. For the purposes of clarification, when we refer to "team" in team leadership, we mean your day-to-day work team and/or any special project teams that you might be temporarily in charge of for your company.

To get you started, the following are some suggestions for building effective teams. These concepts will be discussed in more detail throughout this section.

- Allow time for introductions. When the team is formed, allow people to get to know one another and to clarify roles and goals.

- Show respect for everyone's points of view at the earliest point possible. Try to discourage dominant behaviors by some team members. Research shows that the earliest moments of a team's life define how its members will interact thereafter.

- Establish clear communication channels. Model good listening behavior and encourage it in others. Determine how team members will communicate, how problems will be analyzed, how decisions will be made, and how the team's work will get done.

- Encourage balanced participation early on. To discourage sub-teams from forming, ensure balanced participation and move people around so they interact with everyone else.

- Constructively manage conflict and team difficulties. Do this as soon as the conflicts occur. Never allow a problem to fester.

- Avoid imposing your own ground rules and processes. Instead, let the team decide collectively on their rules for conduct, meetings, and reaching consensus. Research shows that teams that make their own process decisions come together more quickly and are more productive.

As a supervisor, you will be in charge of a team of employees. Your team may include your regular work team or it may also include a special project team created for a short-term purpose. Whether it is your work team or a project team, there are several fundamental principles of team leadership.

A team is a number of persons associated together in work or activity. A team is basically a group of people working towards a common goal. A team can either be made of members selected by a team leader or the team leader may be assigned to an existing team.

The first step towards ensuring a team's success is to look at the abilities, experiences, strengths, and weaknesses of each potential team member. Interview team members to see what types of tasks they have been assigned in the past and then ask for results associated with each task.

Next, look at your own strengths and weaknesses to see how they align with those of your team. Look at the overall project, goals, deliverables, and/or strategies. Finally, select and assign team members based on each member's abilities and according to project requirements, not necessarily on their preferences.

Be a visionary! See beyond the project's endpoint. Communicate the program goals and objectives, the important milestones involved, and the requirements for the deliverables to your team. Discuss and debate the strategies and the metrics for meeting the team's goals/objectives with the team members. Delegate tasks to the team members most qualified to handle them. Rely on them to teach others these tasks when the others are unfamiliar with the tasks. Most importantly, trust your team, being careful not to micromanage them but also being aware of not being too hands off with them. Be there for them when they need your help.

Empower your team members! Have an "open door" policy and allow your team members to make decisions and mistakes without fear of retaliation. Praise your team members when they do well and counsel them when they make mistakes or do wrong. Share the credit, take the blame. By empowering your team they will help you with future endeavors.

Stages in Team Development[2]

Forming. This beginning stage could last a few days or could go on for weeks. People think about their new tasks and their new environment. Members learn about each other and plan their work and their new roles around these new relationships. Emotions are positive. The work team should also learn about team processes in preparation for rough times ahead. They need to learn the rudiments of conflict resolution, communication, time management, and group decision-making.

Storming. The anticipation and enthusiasm of the forming stage quickly fall away as the team faces a myriad of technical, interpersonal, and social problems. They fight and argue. People feel frustration, resentment, and anger as problems fester and work goes undone. Leaders also experience frustration and are tempted to intervene.

Members are on an emotional roller coaster from elation to depression and back again. Without training and support, the team may not progress. Conflict has a bad reputation. But, conflict is normal, natural, and sometimes even necessary. Handled well, conflict can be used to build skills and confidence as the team transitions to the Norming Stage.

Norming. Here, the team works through individual and social issues. They establish their own norms of behavior and begin to trust each other. As the team develops interpersonal skills, it also hones other skills. Members begin to leverage the strengths of each other for the good of the team. They become increasingly adept at problem solving, learning new skills and cross-training each other.

Performing. Now things begin to click. Members help each other, conflict is de-personalized, problems are solved, and goals are achieved and exceeded. Satisfaction and pride become dominant emotions. The team takes pride in their work, pride in their accomplishments, and pride in their team. Individuals take pride in their membership.

Adjourning. Some teams have an end and there can be disappointment and sadness when a team is done and is no longer working together. The loss is real and members should be given time to adjust to their new roles, whether it is an individual role or a new team role.

Team Leadership

A manager is a person who conducts business or a person who directs a team. To manage is to exercise executive, administrative, and supervisory direction; to work upon or try to alter for a purpose; to succeed in accomplishing. Managing is the process of organizing people and tasks to accomplish some purpose.

A leader, however, is a person who leads, or a person who has commanding authority or influence. To lead is to guide in a way especially by going in advance; to guide someone or something along the way. A leader is someone who blazes a trail and takes others along for the ride in order to further a cause.

When you manage, you complete projects and programs through organizing people and tasks in a logical order. Leading means creating a path for others in order to accomplish a greater objective. People lead in order to create a legacy that will be maintained by others for the long run.

You need the qualities of both, a manager and a leader in order to accomplish your projects and programs, and to create a plan for the viability of your organization (develop short-term and a long-range plans). In short, the aim of management is to accomplish tasks, projects, and programs effectively, while leadership aims to help others achieve their personal best.

Learning to Lead

Focus on quality by:

- Setting performance standards
- Outlining realistic goals
- Striving to ensure the highest quality with all objectives
- Maintaining a checklist of your duties and performance of duties

When leading your team, you should:

- Develop strengths — self-confidence and self-determination
- Set high goals

- Eliminate weaknesses — face up to your own mistakes
- Prepare to lead — understand your team members
- Be a strategist

Examine the process — involve everyone in decision making. Conduct a detailed analysis to determine background information. Plan effectively for the team and then implement your plans, both for short and long terms.

To better assess your team and mission, consider a SWOT analysis:

- **S**trengths: What are your competencies? What do you do well?
- **W**eaknesses: What are your shortfalls and competitive disadvantages? What can I improve on?
- **O**pportunities: What is out there that you can take advantage of?
- **T**hreats: What areas are deteriorating? What do you need to be aware of?

Communication

Recognize barriers. People do not always think or hear alike. To achieve clarity with your communications, you should:

- Be clear in your own mind of what you want to communicate?
- Deliver the message clearly using the right media.
- Ensure the message has been clearly and correctly understood as intended.

Principals for People Development

Success in developing others will depend on how well you accomplish each of the following:

- Value of People: Your attitude about others
- Commitment to People: How much time will you give them?
- Integrity with People: Character, or how you treat them
- Standard of People: Vision, or how you see them
- Influence over People: How you lead them

By observing and drawing on the experiences of leaders successful in the area of people development, we learn that there are three main areas in which those who are successful in developing their people differ from those who are not. Successful people developers make the right assumptions about people, ask the right questions, and give the right assistance when needed.

When determining standards for your team, you should:

- Involve employees in developing standards and/or goals and timetables.

- Provide personal examples of top-notch work performance based on which standards can be developed.

- Upgrade performance standards whenever there is a need and an opportunity.

- Make standards measurable so you can determine successful outcomes.

Measures and objectives are important to help chart the direction for your team. They let the team know what it is supposed to be doing. Measures and Objectives are necessary to:

- Monitor and evaluate the use of company resources and the level of controllable costs.

- Establish measurable and realistic work targets and deadlines.

- Monitor performance for any discrepancies that need to be addressed.

- Establish procedures and rules that employees are expected to follow.

- Drive interest in progress toward longer term objectives or goals.

Performance Feedback

Performance feedback is critical to letting your team members know how they are doing. Specifically, performance feedback:

- Lets people know how they are doing on a day by day basis as well as over extended periods of time.

- Is important for coaching and training employees on how to improve performance.

- Is used to determine if goals and objectives are being met.

- Allows employees the opportunity to change their performance.

Performance feedback is an essential element of the supervisor/subordinate relationship. The vast majority of people want to make a difference in their place of work. They want to be recognized for their accomplishments and learn how to become even better. They want to know where they stand. People crave feedback that is honest, positive, objective, timely, and fair. Surprisingly, something as simple and effective as performance feedback is often rare.

There are **three main obstacles** to giving effective feedback in today's leadership environment. The **first** is the pace of operations. Supervisors often say they are so busy that they do not have the time to devote to giving feedback properly. The **second** has to do with working relationships in today's business environment. The good news is that more and more supervisors are taking the time to get to know their subordinates and their families. Their "door is always open." The downside of this is that this type of working relationship can make it hard for supervisors to tell their subordinates that they aren't doing their job well and they could be more effective. The **third** obstacle lies in the willingness and the readiness of the subordinate to receive feedback. Subordinates might have trouble recognizing there are areas in which they can improve. They might be defensive or concerned for their jobs. There might be personality differences or other issues between the supervisor and subordinates that interfere with communication. Effective supervisors must be aware of all the dynamics of the relationship and make appropriate adjustments in their approach to feedback.

A formal feedback process has important advantages for supervisors. It motivates subordinates and helps them become more effective. By establishing dialogue with subordinates, supervisors can better understand their individual wants and needs, and the climate of the organization. In organizations where retaining quality people is a high priority, an effective performance feedback system is essential.

In order for performance feedback to be effective, it must follow these key principles:

Specific: Feedback must be based on observable behavior, not on people's feelings or the conclusions drawn from their behavior. For example, "Last Friday morning I saw you help Mary fix a problem on her computer. Your willingness to share your expertise is a great example of teamwork and makes this a more effective organization." This specific example, tied to a positive organizational outcome, is more effective than saying "You are a helpful person," since the subordinate can link the feedback to an actual event.

Timely: Feedback should be given in a timely enough manner, so that both parties can recall the specific behavior involved.

Actionable: Feedback should be based on something over which a person has control. When necessary, the supervisor should identify ways to improve performance.

Measurable: Goals and objectives should be stated in terms where both parties will know if the goals are achieved.

Achievable: Performance measures should be realistic and within the resources that are available to the subordinate.

Positive: Give both positive and critical feedback, but tip the balance in the positive direction. The Center for Creative Leadership suggests a 4:1 ratio of positive to critical feedback.

Non-evaluative: Opinions, perceptions, and reactions should be differentiated from facts. Don't psychoanalyze; avoid inferences and interpretations. Avoid labels.

Establish a dialogue: The effective feedback session is not a one-way communication. The supervisor should ask the subordinate if he or she fully understands what is being said and then listen carefully to the response. The supervisor should ensure the subordinate understands his or her role in the organization and how that role contributes to the goals and mission of the organization.

When new employees come on board, the supervisor should meet with them as soon after their arrival as possible. The purpose of this initial feedback session is to help establish the relationship between the supervisor and the employee. It is also about setting expectations for the upcoming evaluation period. It is not necessary to negotiate objectives with the subordinate, but the supervisor should help the subordinate take ownership of the goals and internalize expectations. Both parties should leave the initial feedback session with a clear understanding of what is expected. The supervisor provides a written record of the feedback session. This written record is held in confidence.

Supervisors often are required to conduct a follow-up feedback session mid-way through the evaluation period. This session should be conducted using the principles above and should address the extent to which the expectations were met. As before, a confidential written record is provided.

The annual performance appraisal system is not a substitute for good communication within the workplace or for timely routine feedback. For example, if the subordinate is consistently late for routine meetings, it makes no sense to wait until the annual appraisal cycle to make that person aware of the problem. In the same way, workers who consistently perform above standards should not have to wait months to know that their work is appreciated. Supervisors should not assume that, because certain behaviors are obvious to them, they are equally obvious to the subordinate. Daily or routine feedback needs to remain consistent with the principles above.

Annual performance discussions should have no surprises for the employee. The evaluation should summarize the positive and critical feedback given to the employee over a specified time period.

Finally, supervisors who routinely give feedback (both positive and corrective) to subordinates may want to follow up with a personal note or memo. It is possible that the feedback is so routine (or the subordinate so unreceptive) that the subordinate misses the message or doesn't even realize that feedback has taken place.

Giving feedback is a key responsibility of a leader. Work climate surveys strongly suggest that job satisfaction, morale, and retention are closely related to the ability of a leader to provide feedback. Senior leaders must set the example for the organization by giving timely feedback and demanding that leaders at all levels do the same.

The 6 C's of Teamwork

Competence

- Develops and meets standards
- Continuously improves effectiveness through training
- Successfully carries out assignments

- Works together productively
- Strives to increase the level of knowledge concerning individuals, departments, and company issues

Candor

- Honest with each other, encouraging others to speak freely
- Actively listens to the opinions of others with an open mind
- Seeks new ideas and challenges old ones
- Confronts problems and controversial issues assertively

Consensus

- Uses facts to support strong opinions
- Develops innovative solutions together
- Uses a win-win approach to conflict
- Develops excellent solutions and supports final decisions
- Strives for total agreement on important issues

Critique

- Candid, but sensitive to others
- Uses examples and facts as a basis for drawing conclusions
- Focuses on improvements
- Evaluates processes during, as well as after, projects

Cooperation

- Believes we are all in this together
- Involves all members fully

- Shares ideas and information willingly
- Sets challenging goals

Commitment

- Sets rules and then follows them
- Holds self and others accountable
- Seeks team success over individual success
- Commits to following the 6 C's

Seven Keys to Team Leadership

1. ***Help the team identify its purpose.*** People work more effectively when they understand the goals they are trying to achieve. As a leader, it is your job to help the team see the desired outcome of their efforts and help them set specific goals and milestones along the way.

2. ***Set the scope and boundaries.*** Teams need to know what they should tackle and what is "too big" or not their responsibility. By helping teams manage the scope of their work you will keep them more focused and on target to reach the goals more quickly.

3. ***Show, through both your words and actions, that you believe in them.*** If you do not believe in the team concept, you will not effectively lead teams. If you do believe both in the concept and in a particular team's potential, you need to let them know that. Show through both your words and actions that you believe in them. Once they have purpose and goals and your belief in them, they are on their way to success.

4. ***Define your role.*** Your role is to lead, not to do the work or make all of the decisions. Let the team know what your

role is and isn't. Help them see how you are relying on their experience, knowledge and intellect in the completion of the team's work.

5. ***Be a supporter***. Support the team with your actions. Do not just delegate the work to the team and then wipe your hands of any further responsibility. Teams will experience obstacles and road blocks. It is your job to remove those roadblocks, find additional resources, and provide support. It is like a hike. If you are in front of a group on a hike, you will do your best to remove impediments that might slow down or injure those that follow. Your role on a business team of any sort is just the same.

6. ***Be a facilitator***. Help the team succeed. Provide guidance when needed. Remain hands off as much as you can. Let the team succeed and develop themselves towards greater future achievement at the same time. To facilitate means "to make easier," and that is your role. Remember that you chose to use a team to accomplish the task, so let them do it.

7. ***Be careful with what you say***. Teams often look to leaders to make the final decisions or assume that the leader has veto power on any decision in the end. If you really support the team approach, and are genuine in wanting and needing their input, you need to sit back and let them speak. If you are always the first person to talk on a subject, you will slowly stifle their willingness to participate. Team members will subconsciously assume that your word is golden — whether they agree or not. Because of your position, you must abstain from the early part of a dialogue on issues and share your thoughts towards the close of the conversation.

---

2   Adapted from Bruce Thuckman's *1965 model of Forming, Storming, Norming, and Performing.*

Chapter 3
Conflict in the Workplace

Dealing with Team Conflict

The team concept creates an environment where conflict is bound to happen. Dealing with conflict or having difficult discussions with peers or subordinates is not something many people enjoy doing nor are they necessarily trained to do. However, as a supervisor it is essential for you to learn how to handle conflict as it is part of the responsibility of your position. With the right tools you too can learn how to handle these discussions effectively.

Understanding how conflict happens at work can be very helpful for anticipating and fending off situations that may become hostile. While it may seem that conflict can erupt over the slightest of issues in the workplace, the following are the typical reasons why these situations seem to occur.

1. One such cause is incompatible goals between individuals or groups of individuals at work. For example, imagine a bank teller being told by the head teller that rapid service is an absolute must from this point forward, while at the same time the community relation's director instructs all employees to focus their efforts upon quality customer

contact. One can imagine how quickly problems could arise between the teller and the head teller if speed is sacrificed for quality time with the customer.

2. A second source of conflict has to do with our personal values. For example, it does not take long for employees who enjoy going to happy hour after work to begin distancing themselves from those who want to go home to their families at night. Such distancing is often accompanied by gossiping, suspicion, distrust, and ultimately, conflict towards one another.

3. The extent to which we depend upon others to complete our work is a third factor which can contribute to conflict. Certainly conflict would be rare if your task was simply to copy a report on your own copy machine and then file it. However, if you are being pressured to run a report for the records department and find yourself waiting for your turn to use the company copier while the person in front of you spends more time talking than copying, frustration could mount and one could see that the opportunity for conflict begins to expand.

4. Resources as a whole is yet another source of conflict in the workplace. Whether the resource in question involves people, time, money, or things, when we do not have what we need to meet current job demands frustration begins to mount. Ask yourself what happened the last time you were unable to gain access to something you needed at work. Perhaps you experienced some of the "symptoms" that people in such situations experienced.

5. The power distribution at work can be a fifth source of conflict. We have all known people who seem to wield their power inappropriately. Individuals sometimes even inadvertently "step on other people's toes" as they try to complete their own tasks. In addition, there are times when individuals or even entire departments may be viewed as providing a more valuable service to the organization than

do others. In such cases, resentment often arises, laying the foundation for conflict.

6. A final source of conflict to be addressed here has to do with change, and more specifically with changes to company policies and procedures. Some organizations seem notorious for continually changing their policies. Others seem to have no policies at all, or administer them so infrequently that they seem almost non-existent. You may experience this in the form of regular office meetings becoming irregular or being told that you are violating a policy which you thought you were abiding by a week ago, e.g. such as the way you dress. In any case, the absence of clear policies, or policies which are continually changing, creates an environment of uncertainty and subjective interpretation which can leave one feeling vulnerable and helpless.

Confronting Difficult Situations with People

It is always best to confront difficulties at the lowest level in the organization. For example, if you have a conflict with your peers, prepare your case and go talk to them one-on-one to see if you can resolve the conflict. As a supervisor, if an employee comes to you with concerns about a co-worker, the first question you should ask is, "have you spoken to this person yourself about the issue?" If the answer is no, then ask why not. They may need some help in knowing how to approach their peer in a manner that does not make the matter worse. Avoidance is a common tactic used by many in the workplace. The thought is that it will "work itself out." While this may appear to be the simple solution, it is rarely the correct solution.

When a conflict at work requires you to confront an individual, the most effective way is to use what is known as an "assertive" approach. Being assertive does not necessarily mean exerting power and being mean, but it does require effort and practice to put into place, and most find it to be extremely helpful in addressing their needs.

Below are some points you may find helpful to learn and practice before you have to confront an individual:

1. Think ahead about what it is you want to address. What is really bugging you?

2. Set a time to talk with the individual.

3. Deal with only one topic at a time.

4. Be brief and specific.

5. Do not attack the person. Rather, address a specific behavior which the person can recognize and work toward changing (e.g. "I would like you to arrive to work on time," rather than, "I would like you to be more conscientious.")

6. Ask for and listen to their point of view.

In the end, avoiding conflict is simply easier than confronting it. However, this approach does very little towards satisfying your desire to make your workplace a productive and pleasant environment. By better understanding how conflict and anger arise and by practicing how to handle it assertively when it does occur, conflict can become far less intimidating and can actually become an aspect of work you can learn to manage rather than have it manage you.

What to do when conflict happens?[3]

Sometimes the issue at hand evokes strong emotions in you or others involved. When this happens, the C.A.L.M. model can be a great tool used to prepare yourself for confronting another person.

Clarify the Issue

Address the Problem

Listen to the Other Side

Manage Your Way to Resolution

We start with **Clarifying the Issue**. Ask yourself a variety of questions to get a clear understanding of what the issue really is.

Primary Questions

1. What am I upset about? In specific behavioral terms, what actually happened? Who else is involved? What did they do?

2. What emotions am I feeling: anger, hurt, frustration? Why am I feeling this way?

3. Have I contributed to the problem?

4. Am I just overreacting? If so, why?

5. In terms of actions and relationships, what do I desire as far as an outcome to this conflict? What will successful resolution look like?

6. If I were the other person involved in this situation, how would I want to be approached and dealt with?

Secondary Questions

1. Where may the other person have been "coming from"? How might he/she have been motivated by good intentions?

2. Has this happened before? Is this a first-time occurrence?

3. How is this situation affecting me and my work? Are others impacted? If so, how?

4. When dealing with this issue, what can I do to increase my chances of getting the results I want? What counter-productive behaviors do I want to avoid?

Address the Problem: How you open the meeting can be critical. Try to meet in a neutral setting and keep it comfortable for all involved. The tone of voice should be non-accusatory and let the person know you are open for discussion.

The Opening:

I need your help to solve a problem I am facing.

Define the Issue (let them know):

Exactly what happened?

How it made you feel.

The negative impacts the situation has caused.

Other Things to Remember:

Have a walk-in strategy. You may want to practice what you plan to say.

Do not repeat what co-workers have said. This is between the two of you.

Keep the end in mind. The goal is not to win an argument. The goal is to reach a respectful, collaborative result.

Listen to the Other Side: Once you have shared your view, open the discussion and ask for their view. By listening attentively, and without judgment, finding a solution may be easier than you think.

1. Give the other person your total attention.

2. Never interrupt.

3. Ask questions for clarification.

4. Paraphrase what you have heard.

5. Show that you are listening. For example, look them in the eye.

6. Use positive body language.

Manage Your Way to Resolution: When others have shared their view, it is now time to work toward a solution. Do not be too eager to tell them what the solution is or it will make them feel like you have not listened to their viewpoint. Use these tips to find a mutual agreement.

1. Gain an agreement that a problem exists.
2. Identify each other's concerns and needs.
3. Explore win-win solutions.
4. Agree on a course of action.
5. Determine how to handle missteps, should they happen.
6. Close on a positive note.

Managing Team Conflict

It is commonplace for organizations today to work in teams. Whether they be leader-driven or self-directed teams, the hope is that productivity, creativity, and results will be greater in a team environment. While this is a proven approach, any time you bring people together from differing backgrounds and experiences it is inevitable that conflict will occur.

Many people and organizations view conflict as a negative, or something to be avoided. Yet conflict, differences in opinions, and disagreements are a natural result of people working together. Also, without conflict, teams can become complacent and not perform at optimum levels. The challenge then becomes how the team should prepare itself for this stage of their existence and how should the team leader facilitate the team through it.

Conflict arises from a clash of perceptions, goals, or values in an arena where people care about the outcome. If not managed correctly, it can totally disrupt the entire group process. However, the old saying "that which does not kill us will only make us stronger" illustrates how successfully managed conflict can benefit the group.

The best approach to preventing unnecessary conflict is by establishing operating standards and objectives that team members can buy into and support. Then by enforcing your team rules consistently and fairly, you can generally avoid negative conflict.

The first steps in resolving team conflicts are based on an analysis of the team dynamics. This may sound complex and time consuming, but in reality it is a fairly simple process because it is based on assessing the personality types involved. In contrast to overall personality typing, like Myers Briggs, this focuses on the interaction styles of individuals and how they interplay. These styles are accentuated when there is a conflict or a difference in opinions about goals, directions, and plans.

People can be divided into different categories in many ways. When interacting with others, there are varying degrees of extroversion and introversion, aggressiveness, collaboration and competitiveness, and possessiveness. Some people shrink away from conflict and competitiveness. Some are aggressive and see everything as a clash of wills. Some readily compromise by trying to blend their own views and aims with those of others while others simply accept things as they are and have no opinion either way on a matter. In essence, the degrees of give and take, and the feelings of togetherness versus individuality typically dominate team dynamics.

Regardless of which approach is used, teams can surmount many differences and avoid future conflict if it defines common goals and values in the early stages. Goals may seem self-evident, but the motivations which determine the success or failure of these goals are as unique as the individuals themselves.

The overall goal may be to develop a new product, design a new piece of equipment, or create a new report. But the relevance of each task is interpreted differently by each person according to his or her attitudes and perceptions about it. The team can shape plans, set schedules, enact various ways of doing things, and decide upon how the work is reported and recognized so that each person's individual needs and preferences are met.

For example, if a person is individualistic and competitive, then that person's work assignments can be structured as standalone sub-projects completed by him or her, requiring minimal input from others. This allows them to participate as individuals while still being recognized as contributing to the overall team effort. For others, team involvement may be important. Individuals desiring this type of work environment simply thrive better when working in a group. Tasks and efforts are shared in circumstances such as these and responsibility then falls on the shoulders of several individuals instead of a sole member.

Regardless of whether dealing with individuals or with groups, the key thing for a leader to remember when interpersonal conflict does arise is that an open line of communication is usually the best defense toward finding a workable solution. This means creating a safe-zone where employees can voice their opinions and concerns freely and openly with no fear of retaliation.

Doing so often requires a leader to assume the role of a facilitator, or that of a neutral party whose responsibility is to demand mutual respect among team members throughout the resolution process. While you can still encourage, support, and clarify, your most important function in this role is to ensure that team rules and codes of conduct are enforced, both fairly and consistently.

Constructive conflicts exist when ...

1. People change and grow personally from the conflict

2. The conflict results in a solution to a problem

3. Everyone's involvement increases as a result of the conflict

4. It builds cohesiveness among the members of the team

Destructive conflicts exist when ...

1. No decision is reached and the problem still exists
2. It diverts energy away from more value-added activities
3. It destroys the morale of the team members
4. It polarizes or divides the team

Role of Team Leader in Managing Conflict

Organizations and relationships typically fail to mature when conflict is left unresolved. Clearly then, the goal of any leader or manager should be to find a solution equitable to everyone involved. To do so, the two key goals for a group leader are to remain impartial and to facilitate understanding among the group members.

Preventative Strategies

One of the most effective preventative strategies to avoiding conflict is still, the establishment of a good set of ground rules which the team can refer back to for guidance should conflict arise. In addition to outlining processes or behaviors that the group will either allow or prohibit, ground rules can also be used as a way to remove leaders from the role of "enforcer."

Another technique that has been used quite successfully is for the team to come to agreement on how conflict will be resolved when it occurs. This could include, simply reaching a decision by consensus. Most importantly, having a well-defined policy on how conflict will be handled forces the team to focus on behaviors that contribute to it, rather than hamper conflict resolution efforts.

As mentioned previously, training in conflict resolution or communication skills would be invaluable to a team. It would be preferable and most effective if the team could attend this training as a group.

Reactive Strategies

Acting: Exercising an authoritarian approach. Simply tell the group what the resolution will be. This resolves the issue quickly and without discussion. This strategy is best used in emergency situations or when emotions are high and issues will require widespread unpopular decisions. Think through any expected negative fallout ahead of time and have a contingency plan in place. Tell people assertively what it is that you are going to do. Do not hesitate or waffle as this will only add to the confusion.

Adjusting: Splitting differences, exchanging concessions, or "giving and taking" to reach a middle ground. Good when a quick, temporary solution is needed for a complex issue. It merges very different opinions or perspectives quickly. Often a third party mediator is called in to help determine the requirements of all parties. End the mediation by summarizing, gaining commitments, and setting up future check points in the plan.

Accommodating: Sacrificing self-concerns when yielding to another person. Most valuable when one person is more vested in the outcome, when someone is wrong or has made a bad decision, or simply when they have more to gain at a later date. Using the accommodating approach typically requires someone to admit their mistake and then be willing to work toward resolving the matter. Emotions need to be taken out of the picture and there must be discussion as to why one person's giving in is the right thing to do. Then thank them for their willingness to work things out.

Avoiding: Withdrawing, sidestepping or postponing the issue. Most effective when the issue is of low importance or the conflict is a symptom of bigger issues, when you have no decision making authority, or when the issue will resolve itself over time. If using the final approach, make sure you explain why nothing is being done or when you do expect to tackle the issue.

Step-by-Step Process

1. Set expectations. Let all parties know up front that the goal is to resolve the conflict.

2. Make sure all parties want to resolve it.

3. Do not allow for any finger pointing. Let them know there will be no winners or losers. They are all in this together.

4. Clearly identity the reasons for the conflict.

5. Brainstorm solutions that benefit all parties.

6. Get consensus from all parties on the chosen solution.

7. Implement the consented solution.

8. Monitor and evaluate the success/failure of the solution.

9. If successfully resolved — celebrate! If not, go back to step #7.

10. Follow-up and follow-through on any additional requirements.

Resolving Conflict Constructively

Not all conflict and tension is bad. When managed constructively, disagreements can often lead to new ideas, products and best practices, and new ways to do things. Here are seven steps to ensure that conflict is managed constructively:

1. Deflect aggression

   • If the other person is emotional or hostile, remain centered and ignore personal attacks. If that does not work, simply remove that person or yourself from the situation and go through a cooling off period.

   • If others are in conflict, try to calm them down. Again, if that does not work, remove them from the situation while they cool down.

   • Focus on the issues, not the people.

2. Explore the issues
   - Probe to understand each person's point of view.
   - Clarify everyone's assumption.
   - Verify facts and, if needed, gather more information.
3. Listen
   - Give full attention to the person speaking.
   - Paraphrase the other person's point of view.
   - Summarize periodically.
   - Be patient, encouraging the other person to continue until he or she is finished.
   - Try to understand how the other person feels.
4. Acknowledge
   - Recognize the other person by name.
   - Show that you understand and accept the other person's perspective. You do not have to agree with it, but show your awareness.
   - Validate the differences.
5. Solve the Problem
   - Define the problem.
   - Clarify the issues and goals.
   - Find and evaluate alternatives.
   - Determine solution criteria.
   - Apply the criteria and build consensus.
6. Negotiate
   - If problem solving fails, try to negotiate.
   - Find acceptable trade-offs.
   - Determine the impact of trade-offs to each party.
   - Compromise. If that is not possible, submit to arbitration.

7. Assert

- When all else fails, be assertive.
- State your position.
- Express your needs.
- If necessary, agree to disagree.

Resolving Disagreements

Disagreements among team members may not develop into major conflict but can still be disruptive. Here are some suggestions for resolving disagreements:

- Know what is at stake for each person. Ensure that the disagreement is over issues that can be discussed rationally.
- Agree on the issues. Make sure everyone is talking about the same thing.
- Examine assumptions. Other points of view sometimes seem unreasonable because of false assumptions.
- Determine the source of disagreement. Have they interpreted the facts differently? Is there a deeper conflict of values?
- Gather more evidence. Focus on outcomes.
- Have them paraphrase each other's position. This is an excellent technique. Have each person paraphrase the other's position before stating his or her own.
- Suggest that individuals focus on perceptions and share theirs. An opposing position may be less threatening, and certain individuals may find it easier to empathize when it is stated in terms of perceptions: I perceive that ...

Encourage mutual acceptance. If all else fails, suggest that they validate each other's perspective and agree to disagree.

Expect Conflict

At some point in time throughout your leadership journey, you will be exposed to conflict. It is a natural part of life. Whether the conflict involves you or not does not matter. How you handle the conflict will determine your success as a leader.

Complaint Procedures

- Management-designed series of steps for handling employee complaints
- Usually explained in employee handbook or policies
- Usually provides for a number of appeals before a final decision.

---

3 Adapted from *What To Do When Conflict Happens, Participant Workbook (2007)*. Carlsbad, CA: CRM Learning, L.P.

Chapter 4

Recruiting and Selecting your Team

Hiring for Attitude

The hiring patterns you establish today will determine the kind of culture, the kind of service standards, and the kind of reputation you will have tomorrow.

The proposition is undeniable. You cannot build a great company without great people. How many companies are as rigorous about hiring or as comfortable evaluating job candidates as they are about deciding on an investment proposal or deciding which contractor company to hire? The all-too-common reality in companies is that hiring processes are poorly designed and executed.

Of course, making the commitment to hire great people raises an even more basic question. How do you know them when you see them? Over the last few years, a number of companies have asked themselves that question. They have analyzed what separates their winners from their losers, good hires from bad hires. These companies compete in a wide range of industries — from airlines to steel, computers to hotels — but they all arrived at the same answer: What people know is less important than who they are. Hiring, they believe, is not about finding people with the right experience. It is about finding people with the right mind-set. These companies hire for attitude and train for skill.

The same can be said for promotions and advancement within an organization. All too often employees are promoted into supervisory positions because they have demonstrated excellence in their work or because they have been there for a long time. As supervisors, now they deal with people and their needs instead of simply production needs. Are we really setting these employees up for success if we only promote based on technical competency?

Do not get the wrong idea. Just because we need to look beyond technical skills when hiring does not mean that we need to become amateur psychologists. It simply means that the hiring process should be set to the same rigorous standards as those used when making any other strategic decision within the company.

Hire for Attitude, Train for Skill

Truth #1: Most organizations hire for technical competence and expertise, hoping that the technically gifted will bring the right attitude with them.

Truth #2: You will hire people for what they know and what they can do. You will most often fire people for who they are.

Truth #3: What people know is less important than who they are. What we know changes very fast in an information-based world. Who we are, changes over a long period of time.

Truth #4: Hiring someone with a bad or marginal attitude, but who is technically competent, and then expecting the Training Department to change them is a decision you will pay for over and over again.

Truth #5: When you have fewer people doing more work you cannot afford to make a sloppy hiring decision.

Truth #6: The most admired companies in the world are absolutely rigorous about hiring — it is a strategic priority for them. They know the price they will pay for "just filling a position."

The New Model For Smart Hiring

1. *What You Know Changes, Who You Are Does Not*

   Popeye (Popeye the "Sailor Man" is an American cartoon fictional character created by Elzie Crisler Segar in 1930s) was right: "I y'am what I y'am." The most common — and fatal — hiring mistake is to find someone with the right skills but the wrong mind-set and hire them on the theory, "We can change 'em." Forget it. The single best predictor of future behavior is past behavior.

2. *You Cannot Find What You are Not Looking For*

   There are several dimensions for success on the job, including practical learning, teamwork, tolerance for stress, sales ability, attention to detail, adaptability, flexibility, and motivation, just to name a few. If you are not actively looking for these traits and skills, you will not find them.

3. *You Cannot Hire People Who Do Not Apply*

   Companies that take hiring seriously also take recruiting seriously. Successful companies seldom lack job candidates. The goal is to have the right job candidates, not the most. Another approach to recruiting builds on the theory that blood is thicker than water. Most companies with advanced hiring systems encourage family members to apply for jobs. The logic is simple. If "who people are" is what matters, who better to hire than people related to your top performers? Another option is to encourage employees to recommend candidates — again our friends, with values similar to ours.

Why Quality Recruiting and Selection Matters

The hiring and selection patterns you establish today will determine the kind of culture, the kind of service standards, and the kind of reputation you have tomorrow. Will it be a culture you are excited about or one you simply tolerate? Will it be a reputation you are proud of or one for which you are always making excuses?

What you know will change through experience, education, and on-the-job training, but who you are is less likely to change as fast. So hiring someone with the hope that you can change their core character and the fundamental values that shape their attitude when they come to work for you is a bad hiring decision. Many marriages fail today for the same reason. We like some things but not everything about our potential spouse, and we hope that when we finally tie the knot we can change them! But we all know how flawed that thinking is (either through our own personal experience or through knowing someone who has tried it and failed).

Finally, in a world with limited resources and more work than ever, we cannot afford to make hiring mistakes. There is a finite amount of time in each day. We can either waste part of that time on personnel problems that emanate from bad hiring decisions, or we can get the most out of that time on things that add value for our customers and widen the gap of competitive advantage.

Why is it difficult to hire the best?

Perhaps it is difficult to hire the best because we have not been through the rigorous process of defining what the best looks like. Hiring people with world-class attitudes starts with identifying the people in your own organization who already have the kind of attributes you want. Find the superstars in your company. Ask their customers, employees, peers, and supervisors what makes them so effective, so easy to work with, and so competent. Then build a profile of the common denominators that make each superstar successful and hire new people based on those attitudinal profiles.

Hiring is a pay-me-now or pay-me-later endeavor. If you invest the time up front to critically think through what attitudes, characteristics and values you want, and then hire accordingly, the rewards can be invaluable. If, on the other hand, you are lazy or impatient, the negative consequences can be disastrous. We all know through experience that "attitudes are contagious." As you interview people for future positions, ask yourself, "Is theirs worth catching?"

While you are at it, why not ask yourself the same question, "Is my attitude worth catching?" As a leader, you are an ambassador for your organization. You have the power to set the tone for your organization's success in recruiting, screening, and hiring world-class people with world-class attitudes. What kind of legacy are you building?

Developing a Recruiting and Selection Strategy

In order to be successful, organizations must have the ability to locate, identify, and attract qualified candidates. Recruiting involves much more than placing an employment ad in the paper — an effective recruitment program serves as a foundation for meeting current and future staffing requirements. Incorporating a recruiting strategy that is both systematic and creative provides the innovation and cost effectiveness needed to remain competitive in any business environment.

The recruiting process involves six key steps:

1. Establish the organization's recruiting objectives
2. Identify the position requirements and opportunities
3. Evaluate the recruiting climate and response
4. Determine appropriate sources

5. Implement the recruiting campaign

6. Monitor the results

Your Missions, Vision, and Values

You should incorporate your organization's Mission, Vision, and Values into the selection process. This can be done by including questions during the interview that determine if the candidate is the right person for the job and would be a good fit for your company.

Such questions might include:

- How would you best contribute to our company's mission of ...?

- Tell us about a time when you specifically had to choose the company's interests over those of your own.

- One of our key values is _____. What skills or talents do you have that can help us with supporting this value?

The point here is that the person you hire should be able to support your Mission, Vision, and Values. Otherwise, the person will not be a good fit for your company.

Additionally, you should consider incorporating your values into your performance appraisal process and then rating employees on their performance relative to supporting those values.

Determining Recruiting or Selection Objectives

To determine specific recruiting objectives, start by linking to the organization's business plan along with evaluating past staffing patterns, current and future hiring needs, and budget restrictions. To arrive at these objectives, consider the following:

Organization's Business Plan

What is the organization's plan and focus over the next few years? What kind of employees are needed to meet the organization's needs? If you are selecting team members from an existing pool of employees, what are the team's objectives and what skills are needed to successfully accomplish those objectives?

Long Term vs. Short Term Employment Strategic Plan

What are the long term and short term needs? Considerations include property acquisitions, downsizing, and expansion.

Position and Team Requirements

Position requirements would entail assessing the essential duties and responsibilities of the job, the type and degree of expertise needed, the kind of decision making required, and the amount of time spent performing each function. Cultural fit factors look at how work is accomplished in an organization. For example, the degree of formality and use of set procedures, the pace and amount of change, and the extent of team versus individual work focus are just a few.

The same considerations should be used when selecting team members. In addition, consider the overall skills and abilities of each team member. For a team to be well rounded and perform at its best, look for the strengths each member brings to the table and build upon them. For example, select members who are detail oriented as well as those who are task driven. Look for members who focus on logic and data as well as those who look at the impact decisions will have on people. Good communications, strong listening skills, the ability to work through conflicting points of view, and adaptability are highly prized in all members of the team.

Bad hiring selections often end up costing organizations a great deal of time and money and are usually the result of poorly defined or inadequately communicated job requirements. Unrealistic requirements limit the available candidate pool and restrict recruiting efforts. In addition, the amount of training the company will provide for the position is important in determining the level of experience and job knowledge needed for an employee new to the job as opposed to employees who have been in the job for a period of time.

Reviewing the Resume and Job Application

Reviewing resumes is a critical part of the overall hiring process and is an area where many companies fail to devote enough time. As a result, they either end up with a poor choice or miss an opportunity with a shooting star.

Resume screening is the process of comparing one candidate's qualifications to another's or comparing a candidate's skills and abilities to the requirements of the job. This, again, is an integral part of the hiring process making it essential for an organization to allocate both time and resources for this. In addition, in this day of electronic applications, resume screening has taken on several new dimensions.

Before the age of electronics, resume screening could be as simple as looking at the design of the document, the quality of the paper used for printing or the size of the envelope it was mailed in. While still useful for those resumes mailed in, electronic applications have become more of the norm now and with that comes a whole new set of screening requirements and challenges. However, there is still one thing that never goes out of style regardless of whether submitted by pen on paper or transmitted through electronic gadgetry, and that is proper spelling and grammar. Potential candidates who fail to give adequate attention to details such as these do not warrant the time and effort involved in reviewing their application.

Steps In Resume Review

1. Resumes should include a cover letter. Review the cover thoroughly before proceeding to the actual resume itself. The cover letter typically tells you a lot about a potential

candidate, including why they want to come to work for you, their goals and aspirations, and what they expect from you, if hired. If the resume you are reviewing has no cover letter included, it should be a red flag that not a lot of effort was put forth on the part of the applicant. Depending on the nature of the position you are looking to fill, you will need to decide at this point whether or not to continue reviewing the resume.

2. Scan the resume to obtain an overall impression of the applicant. Look especially for a flawless presentation, correct spelling and grammar, and their attention to detail. Paper resumes must pass the "feel" test.

3. In the first skim, look for the easy-to-find qualifications. If you are requiring a college degree and they do not have one, reject the resume or place it in your "maybe" meets qualifications pile or electronic folder.

4. Read the section in the cover letter or resume where the candidate tells you what they are looking for in a job. If your job posting stated specific qualifications and the potential candidate simply stated they are looking for a "challenging environment," this, again, is a red flag that not much effort was put forth in applying for the job. This could be an indicator of the type of work ethic they would employ if hired.

5. Look at the applicant's list of qualifications and experiences to see if they align with the requirements of the job. Again, if the applicant has taken the time to "customize" their summary to your needs, you should easily be able to make the connection as to whether or not they have the aptitude and skills you are looking for.

6. Next, take a look at where the applicant worked in the past. Look for accomplishments and any contributions made while working for previous or current employers. Be aware of anything that specifically relates to the job

requirements of the position you are looking to fill. Look for key words which can tie their past experiences to your current needs. Finally, look for any red flag items including the following:

- Employment gaps
- Evidence of decreasing responsibility
- Evidence of a career that has reached a plateau or gone backwards
- Short term employment at several jobs
- Multiple shifts in career path

A word of caution here. As you review resumes for the above listed items, be aware of generational differences: the values and work ethics attributed to the different generations. A baby boomer may see someone who frequently changes jobs as a "job hopper" or someone "not able to hold a job." On the other hand, a Gen Y'er may see the same person as someone "expanding their horizons" or making themselves more marketable. Be aware of these differences and do not allow for "mental stereotyping" as you continue with your resume review.

7. If in doubt, check it out. Applicants should always include a list of references with their resume. Do not be afraid to call those people listed as references and ask questions if there are things about the candidate you would like more information about.

8. Finally, schedule interviews with those candidates who have passed your initial screening process.

Remember, the more you review resumes, the better your resume review will become. With practice, your resume review should yield great candidates for you to consider for future employment.

In closing, please review the following Checklist for Reviewing Resumes or Application Forms.

Checklist for Reviewing Resumes or Application Forms

Sort applicants by job for which they are applying. Save miscellaneous applications for last.

- Review the job description(s) for the position(s) you are attempting to fill. Note minimum requirements needed and refer to them often as you review resumes/applications.

- Ignore the applicant's name, address or personal information to limit subconscious biases.

- Attempt to ignore superficial issues such as style and typographical areas in favor of content unless such issues are directly related to the position for which they are applying. Such scrutiny may unintentionally rule out members of protected classes.

- Check work experience for applicability to the position for which they are applying, length of time they have worked in similar areas, promotions or awards received, and reasons for leaving.

- Note gaps in employment but do not assume they were caused by negative reasons.

- Check educational background for qualifications necessary to have successful job performance.

- Note special skills (i.e. computer software, office equipment).

- Note on a separate piece of paper any pertinent questions that arise when reviewing the resume/application and ask those during your initial contact with the prospect.

- Divide resumes into 3 groups — one for those that closely match job requirements and for which a preliminary contact is appropriate, one for those who meet some requirements and may be considered at some point, and one for those who do not meet the requirements at all.

- If necessary, screen the top group again to further narrow down the candidates. On average, about 10 resumes per open position should be sufficient.

During your initial contact with them, briefly describe the position, location, hours and salary range (if appropriate) and ask if the candidate is still interested in being considered. If so, this is the time to ask for clarification on any items you had questions about when reviewing their resume.

Hire the Most Qualified Applicant Using a Fair and Non-discriminatory Process

- Review the selection process to ensure that you treat each applicant fairly and consistently.

- Review the interview format and questions for possible bias. Consult with your HR group as well as others trained in the hiring process. Then review the process with your recruiting team to ensure there are no questions that are biased and prejudicial. Discuss the impact of common biases such as stereotyping, unsubstantiated first impressions that may influence a decision, and assessments based on differing "comfort levels" with them. Reaffirm the fact that decisions must be made on facts and not on perceptions.

- Ensure that reasonable accommodations are made for the applicants, such as ensuring the handicapped access is available for an applicant in a wheelchair.

- If using a group interview process, create a diverse selection panel.

- Assess all candidates using the same selection criteria.

- Interview as many applicants as possible to increase the pool from which you will have to choose. Use competency-based interviewing techniques.

- Eliminate interview questions that are not job related.

- Keep written records of all applicants interviewed and be certain that the information saved is relevant to the applicant's ability to perform the required duties and are not simply personal opinions.

- Follow-up with references after the interview and ask job-related questions about the applicant's knowledge, skills, and ability to do the job. Document questions and answers.

- Be consistent with reference checks. Weigh information received consistently for all applicants.

- Give all applicants an opportunity to address any negative feedback from reference checks.

- Document the selection process fully. Retain all records: interview questions, notes, reference check questions and notes, and the completed Interview Assessment forms.

Background Checks and Reference Checks

Employers can check for criminal records when conducting employment background checks, but state laws limit the extent to which employers can use these when making hiring decisions. Examples of such decisions include the refusal to hire or promote based solely on their criminal record.

Restrictions concerning the use of criminal records are imposed by state and federal laws and by guidelines established by state government agencies and civil rights organizations. Restrictions vary by state. But, overall:

- Employers usually can not disqualify job candidates solely on the grounds they have criminal records.

- Employers typically may not ask about or consider a juvenile criminal record to make job or other employment related decisions.

- Employers typically have the right to ask about and conduct an adult criminal record search to make job or other employment decisions.

- Employment decisions about whether or not to hire should be limited to convictions only. Just because an applicant may be charged with a felony does not make them automatically guilty.

- Employers must show that an applicant's conviction would have an impact on an applicant's suitability to fill a position before the employer can make a hiring decision based solely on the conviction. An applicant with a criminal history of child abuse would not be a good fit for a job in a day care center.

Again, restrictions vary by state. Some are very rigid in what they allow and do not allow while others may have no restrictions whatsoever. Regardless, the United States Equal Employment Opportunity Commission (EEOC) has imposed very specific employment discrimination laws which are very broad in nature and sometimes very loosely defined.

For example, if an employer does not hire an applicant because of the specifics of their criminal record, the EEOC could still constitute that employment discrimination has occurred if that applicant were a member of an ethnic group. It is important to remember that you must have a justifiable business reason to deny employment if criminal background is involved. If you have any questions about this, or just are not sure, contact your local EEOC field office for more information.

A note of importance — some states require certain employers to conduct criminal record checks for specific convictions before hiring employees. Employers required to conduct criminal record checks are typically engaged in businesses that involve so-called vulnerable individuals such as children and elderly adults. Examples include childcare, education, and home healthcare.

Pre-Employment Inquiries

USA federal law requires employers to conduct the applicant screening and hiring process in a non-discriminatory manner. Pre-employment inquiries (on application forms, by telephone, in interviews) can be considered illegal if they screen out women, minorities or other protected groups. As a result, the Equal Employment Opportunity Commission (EEOC) cautions that inquiries concerning an applicant's race, color, religion, or national origin may be regarded as discriminatory.

Exceptions: Pre-employment inquiries are permissible if required by local, state, or federal law. They are also allowed when religion and national origins are bona fide occupational qualifications (BFOQs), or where the employer can prove that the inquiry is justified by business necessity and is job-related.

Reference Checks

In addition to contacting former employers and personal references, many organizations expand the selection process to include checks for driving records, education, and other professional credentials and credit history. In general, the following rules apply:

- Check federal, state and local laws and regulations before proceeding.

- Be certain there is a job or business-related reason for the selection processes utilized (i.e., motor vehicle checks for drivers, credit checks for bank tellers.)

- Explain the procedures on the application form, in the interview, or wherever appropriate.

- Have the applicant sign an authorization form for each of the types of information to be checked. Legal counsel can assist with proper wording.

- There are numerous firms that provide assistance with background checks. Be certain they are reputable and comply with all federal, state and local laws.

- Maintain confidentiality.

Other Legal Considerations

Every country has employment laws that govern the "do's and do not's" of recruiting and interviewing. Although we have highlighted some areas that all leaders should be aware of, this is not a complete list of legal considerations. A good Human Resource person or employment attorney can be a huge asset to ensure your processes and procedures keep you out of court.

Developing the Interview and Questions

Respect the Candidate

Valuing candidate's time can be one of the most important drivers in the interview process.

1. The interview schedule should meet candidate and interview team needs to the extent possible.

2. Try to minimize follow-up interviews for candidates as much as possible (particularly out-of-town applicants). Web-based preliminary interviews are particularly helpful and convenient for out-of-town candidates.

3. Make sure that every member on your interview team starts on and ends the interview on time. Schedule a 15 minute buffer between interviews in the event one of them runs long or a candidate shows up late.

4. Make sure you schedule a lunch break for your interview team so they can relax and re-energize. If possible, have the team eat together so they can discuss the events for the morning.

5. Keep the number of interviews to a manageable number.

6. Ensure all interviewers have a copy of the candidate's resume in advance.

7. Appoint an individual to be the point person for the candidate.

8. Provide the candidate with a follow-up timeline, or what will happen next.

We want candidates to feel their time has been well spent. When the candidate leaves, they should have clear expectations about the next step and a very positive impression of the organization.

Once interviews have been completed, the interview team should meet to discuss the candidates and make a selection decision. This should be done as soon as the interview team is able.

If the decision is to extend an offer, work with appropriate staff to develop the offer and convey it to the candidate.

If the decision is a "no hire" decision, communicate this to the candidate. Be sure to communicate in a timely fashion.

If the decision is to hold on the candidate (not offer but not reject), someone on the interview team should contact the candidate to let them know they are a viable candidate and what to expect next. Sometimes you may hold a candidate until your top candidate accepts the job offer or until additional candidates have been interviewed.

Core Competencies: Behavioral Definitions

Adaptability:

- Seek, understand, and accept change.
- Treat change and new situations as opportunities for learning or growing.
- Focus on the beneficial aspects of change.
- Speak positively about the change to others.
- Modify behavior to deal effectively with changes in the work environment.
- Try new approaches for new situations.

Teamwork:

- Value, appreciate, and include others.
- Place team or organizational goals ahead of personal goals.
- Help others achieve mutual goals.
- Exchange ideas freely and then build on them.
- Get team consensus on ideas and then take action on them.

Integrity:

- Be honest and forthright.
- Present information accurately and completely.
- Keep commitments.
- Keep confidences.
- Be consistent with words and actions.
- Represent organizational strengths and abilities fairly and equitably.

Initiative:

- Take thoughtful, yet timely action when confronted with a problem or difficult situation.

- Implement new ideas or solutions without being prompted.

- Be an overachiever. Go above and beyond basic job requirements in order to achieve goals.

- Seek opportunities to improve efficiencies and reduce costs.

Innovation:

- Identify alternate ways to view or define problems.

- Use as many diverse sources for ideas and inspiration as you can find.

- Brainstorm ideas.

- Consider multiple solutions.

- Target areas for innovation.

Functional Competencies: Behavioral Definitions

Accounting and Finance:

- Prepare cost projections for new and existing products and submit them in a monthly report to your manager.

- Ensure inventory accounts are properly funded on a monthly basis.

Administrative:

- Prepare and/or coordinate such things as travel arrangements, presentations, meetings, and other functions as requested by manager.

- Enter all necessary data into the books, and then review and reconcile the books on a monthly basis to ensure that all invoices are submitted and/or paid prior to due dates.

Engineering:

- Design, write, and execute standard protocols.

- Support manufacturing through continuous process/ product improvement efforts.

Human Resource:

- Analyze data in regards to turnover, cost per hire, compensation, benefits, and affirmative action relative to industry trends. Report findings to management on a monthly basis.

- Monitor the effectiveness of all policies and procedures to ensure compliance. Support and broaden the diversity of your workforce through both your hiring and your promotion efforts.

Information Technology:

- Prioritize and manage Information System projects to assure they are on time and on budget. If the project involves new hardware or software, ask for feedback from users to ensure everything is running as expected and they are properly trained on the use of the new products.

- Monitor network performance for problems on a daily basis.

Warehouse Operations:

- Check incoming procurements against requisitions, shipping memos, packing slips, invoices, and/or freight bills to assure that all orders are received in full and arrived in good condition. Also, make sure that all outgoing sales and orders are packaged and shipped in a timely manner. If inconsistencies are found in either incoming or outgoing products, report them to management on the shift on which they were found.

- Read and understand all rules and regulations pertaining to warehouse management, especially those related to the occupational safety and health hazard related issues.

Production:

- Check product/production outputs for accuracy, quality, and quantity on a daily, sometimes even an hourly basis. If there are negative variances, try to determine the cause.

- Ensure that all equipment is properly set up and in safe working condition on a shift by shift basis. Report any deficiencies immediately.

- Provide operator training on all equipment and then monitor performance to ensure proficiency and abilities.

Quality/Regulatory Affairs:

- Periodically conduct quality assurance checks. This includes checking incoming materials, work in progress, and finished goods. Ensure that all work being done is according to well defined criteria and follows rules and regulations defined by regulatory agencies.

- Analyze all data received and communicate results to your management team. Look for any gaps in expected outcomes. Then create and assign action plans to ensure corrections are made.

Research and Development:

- Develop tactics and strategies that encourage the development and launch of new products and services. Conduct marketing surveys to find what customers want and need. Share success stories at monthly department meetings.

Sales and Marketing:

- Develop and implement strategies and tactical plans to achieve current and long-range sales goals for assigned products. Communicate these to management on a quarterly basis.

- Modify proposals or plans to deal with customer's concerns and incorporate customer's suggestions on an on-going basis.

Scientific/Medical:

- Coordinate input, collaboration, and consultation for the design of clinical protocols and submissions to ensure the proper product indications are supported. Ensure medical and scientific protocol validity.

- Generate sound scientific data by identifying and solving problems, planning and taking the lead on assigned development projects, writing and reviewing scientific reports, and performing laboratory activities.

Leadership Competencies: Behavioral Definitions

Build Our Organization and Inspire Our People:

- Determine and acquire, or develop, the knowledge, skills, and abilities needed to achieve the organization's goals.

- Staff the organization from various disciplines, backgrounds, and cultures to promote and capitalize on diversity and to ensure complementary talents and skills.

- Create a committed and productive organization that acts with integrity.

- Establish clear expectations and provide timely,

accurate feedback, both positive and negative. Take appropriate follow-up action when needed.

- Recognize, reward, and promote people based on their performance, achievements, and development of competencies.
- Serve as a role model.

Set Vision and Strategy:

- Understand trends, their implications, and opportunities in the global environment.
- Maintain a strong customer focus.
- Identify and capitalize upon opportunities to create value from cross-division capabilities.
- Effectively communicate the business vision and strategies to all in the organization.
- Look to the future using the global marketplace, technology, and business knowledge to identify emerging opportunities, and then seize them.
- Effectively translate the business vision and broad strategies into concrete, actionable strategic plans and goals, prioritizing goals, projects, and plans appropriately.

Encourage Open Exchange of Ideas and Knowledge:

- Foster a work environment that encourages open communication and knowledge sharing, leveraging that sharing to drive continuous improvement and positive outcomes.
- Encourage the expression of opposing and differing points of view.
- Practice effective listening skills.
- Listen and think about diverse or differing ideas before responding.

- Proactively seek feedback and demonstrate a willingness to learn and change.

- Give honest, timely feedback, both positive and critical, to staff as well as higher level management.

Know the Business:

- Continuously scan the environment, identifying key issues, trends, relationships, and cause/effect as they impact the business.

- Learn from and build on business experience to ensure success.

- Demonstrate a strong personal capability for learning new aspects of the business and encourage others to do the same.

Drive for Results:

- Collaboratively set realistic, challenging, measurable goals and timetables.

- Set short-term objectives that drive longer-term goals or strategies.

- Support staff with necessary resources to achieve goals.

- Hold yourself and others accountable for delivering high quality results.

- Regularly evaluate yourself and your team on goal attainment, the process used to achieve goals and competitive benchmarks.

- Be tenacious.

Make the Difficult Decisions:

- Demonstrate the willingness to make and accept unpopular decisions or take opposing positions.

- Challenge the status quo on traditional ways of doing things.

- Recognize signs of crisis situations and take corrective action at the earliest indication of trouble.

- Recognize errors and make corrections as necessary.

- Make the difficult people decisions when needed.

General Guidelines for Choosing Questions

Using behavior based questions is an effective way to learn how the candidate has responded in the past. Since past behavior is the best predictor of future behavior, we highly suggest using behavior based questions. Although situational questions can be useful, candidates can often give you a textbook answer without ever having been in the situation themselves.

A behavior based question is an open ended question that causes the candidate to discuss how he/she has responded to a situation in the past. Each question asks the candidate to evaluate:

1. A positive situation/task

2. A negative situation/task

3. A situation/task with a subordinate, co-worker, supervisor or customer.

Choose questions for each competency that you are seeking for a particular position. Make sure you address each type of question for each competency. By looking at questions from various perspectives, you will gain further insight into personality factors as revealed through behaviors.

How to Create Your Own Behavior-Based Interview Question
Sometimes, particularly with functional competencies, you will need to create your own behavior-based questions. Following

the steps below, you will be able to create legal and behaviorally orientated questions in no time.

Remember, the point of the question is to use the past to help predict the future.

1. Begin by identifying the position's behavior and related competency.

2. A good way to start a question is with one of the following phrases "Describe a time, situation, action ..." "Tell me about ..." "Give an example of ..." or "Provide an example of a situation when ..."

3. When choosing your words, use terminology specific to the position.

4. Get to the heart of the matter quickly — questions should be no more than one to two sentences.

5. Avoid creating a scenario for the candidate. Words that indicate you are doing this include "like," "for example," and "for instance."

6. Review your questions to ensure that they are legal.

7. Remember, if it is not job related, it is not relevant.

8. Human Resources should review any questions you create.

Beyond the First Behavioral Question

A good behavioral-based question will accomplish two things: 1) get the candidate talking and 2) give you an opportunity to see how the candidate acted or reacted. Your job is not done after you ask the first question, though. Sometimes you will need more information. Remember that all behavior-based interview questions seek a STAR within the answer. S/T is the situation/task; A is the action the candidate took in that instance; R is the result. When using the STAR method, ask questions starting with "How," "What," "When," "Where," and "Why."

Do not hesitate to ask for the outcome in both subjective and objective forms. If the candidate cannot think of a time they experienced a situation or task, do not let them speculate on how they may have responded. Suggest a scenario or two to jog their memory. If they still cannot think of a situation, move on to the next question. This tells you something about them that is helpful.

Core Competencies and Corresponding Questions

Listed below are the core competencies we described earlier to you along with some behavior based questions/situations which can be used as examples to help you build your own questions.

Adaptability:

- Describe a time when you came up with a new process while in your position.

- Describe a time when you had to change your thinking when you really did not want to or did not agree with what was being proposed.

Teamwork:

- Give an example of a time when you encouraged a more reserved member of the team to contribute to the sharing of ideas.

- Give an example of a time when you put your personal interests aside in order to recognize the achievement of a team member or the organization.

- Tell about a time when you supported an organization's decisions even though you felt as though there were better alternatives.

Integrity:

- Tell about a time when you were asked to do something that you believed was not right.

- Describe a time when you were asked to provide a customer with a product or service that was not truly needed.

- Describe a time when you were given full credit for a job when there were actually others who had contributed significantly to the outcomes.

Initiative:

- Explain the manner in which you handled a difficult situation with a customer.

- Describe a time when you identified a small problem before it became a big problem.

- Give an example of a new idea you came up with and presented without the prompting of your supervisor.

Innovation:

- Describe a time when you came up with a new way of looking at things.

- Give one or two examples of changes you have made to the way things used to be done prior to your moving into your current position.

- Give an example of an unusual place you found information that has helped you on the job.

Chapter 5
Leadership Communications

Communications

Effective communication is ESSENTIAL to being successful in the workplace. The biggest cause of workplace problems is poor communications. The key to the communication process is to be *understood*.

Functions of Communication

1. Convey ideas, concepts, plans, procedures, work requirements, etc.

2. Motivate, inspire, and direct performance in others.

3. Provide a release for concerns, problems, issues, and workplace conflict.

4. Provide information needed to make informed decisions.

Communication Goals

The aim of communication is the transference and understanding of information between two or more people.

Communication must always be between two or more people. There is always a sender and a receiver. You participate in both roles and your role will change alternatively and frequently throughout the conversation.

Effective communication has occurred only when the message sent has been understood in the mind of the receiver. Feedback is critical to ensuring that the message has been accurately received and understood.

Six Barriers to Effective Communication

1. *Filtering:* A sender's manipulation of information so that it will be seen more favorably by the receiver.

2. *Selective Perception:* People selectively interpret what they see on the basis of their interests, background, experience, and attitudes.

3. *Information Overload:* A condition in which information inflow exceeds an individual's processing capacity.

4. *Emotions:* How a receiver feels at the time a message is received will influence how the message is interpreted.

5. *Language:* Words have different meanings to different people.

6. *Communication Apprehension:* Undue tension and anxiety about oral communication, written communication, or both.

A Good Communicator:

- Seeks out and is receptive to input from others.

- Uses a variety of questioning techniques to gain insight and participation into conversation.

- Practices active listening.

- Channels information upward, downward, and laterally.

- Coordinates with all other leaders, peers, superiors, and subordinates.

- Consistently reviews daily operations and provides feedback and/or instructions.

- Uses a variety of communication vehicles and chooses the most appropriate vehicle(s) and/or style(s) for a given situation.

- Effectively presents ideas to work group members.

- Explains the "why" behind work assignments and activities/policies that impact the work group or individual employees.

- Identifies and resolves communication problems between group members including when it involves them.

Active Listening

Active listening is a communication technique that reduces defensiveness and loss of self-esteem, and acts to defuse an emotional exchange. The term "active listening" means the ability to pick up, define, and respond accurately to the feelings expressed by the other person. When active listening is employed, people perceive that they are being understood.

When you fail to listen well, you risk:
- Misreading people's intentions
- Misinterpreting ideas
- Confusing the issue
- Misjudging people's qualifications
- Misunderstanding instructions
- Jumping to the wrong conclusions
- Antagonizing people

The Four Steps of Active Listening

1. *Listen:* To feelings as well as to words, emotions, and implications. Focus on the speaker. Look at them. Use verbal and non-verbal encouraging signs to let them know you are listening to them. Do not plan what to say or get distracted while listening.

2. *Question:* Demonstrates you are listening. Use to gather information and to obtain clarification. Ask open-ended questions such as "Tell me more," "How did you feel," or "Then what happened?"

3. *Reflect-Paraphrase:* In your own words, reflect what is said and the feelings expressed, reframe to capture the essence of the communication, remove negative framing, and move toward problem solving.

4. *Agree:* Get speaker's consent to your reframing. This lets the speaker know they have been heard. Let them know that a solution is near!

Climbing the LADDER — to better listening

LOOK at the speaker — Meanings are not in the words, but in the people.

ASK questions — The quickest way to become a listener.

DO NOT interrupt — It is just as rude to step on people's ideas as it is to step on their toes.

DO NOT change the subject — Listening means wanting to hear.

EMOTIONS — Leaders should be aware of their own emotions, and be aware of the emotional undercurrents in the environment. Emotions create a storm and others will back away.

RESPONSIVE listening — When people feel that their leader no longer listens or responds, they will go somewhere else.

Giving and Receiving Feedback

10 Common Performance Feedback Mistakes

1. Speaking out only when things are wrong. "Praise to a human being represents what sunlight, water and soil are to a plant — the climate in which one grows best." — Earl Nightingale

2. "Drive-by" praise without specifics or an honest underpinning. — "Great job!"

3. Waiting until performance or behavior is substantially below expectations before acting on it.

4. Giving positive or negative feedback long after the event has occurred.

5. Not taking responsibility for your thoughts, feelings, actions, and reactions. "This comes straight from the boss."

6. Giving feedback through e-mail messages, notes, or over the telephone.

7. Giving negative feedback in public.

8. Criticizing performance without giving suggestions for improvement.

9. No follow up afterwards.

10. Not having regularly scheduled performance review meetings.

Four Tips for Effective Performance Feedback

1. *Be proactive.* Nip issues in the bud and avoid the messy interpersonal tangles that result from neglected communication. Meet with employees on a monthly or quarterly basis instead of annually. This lets them know that they are important to you and you care about their success.

2. *Be specific.* It is never easy to provide negative feedback regarding someone's work, but as a leader you cannot avoid

it. Be as clear as possible when providing feedback (both positive and negative). Give specific examples that illustrate your points. For example, instead of saying, "Your attitude is bad" or "That did not work," you might say something like, "When you miss deadlines, then cross your arms and look away when I discuss it with you, it gives me the impression that you do not care about the quality of your work. I'd like to believe this isn't true. Can you help me explain this better?"

3. *Develop a progress plan.* Tell them what specifically needs to change and when that change needs to occur. Schedule follow-ups to check on progress and then make sure you follow-up as scheduled.

4. *Link employee performance to organizational goals.* Reinforce the value of your employees' contributions by giving specific examples of how their work and positive behaviors serve the organization and its customers.

Receiving Feedback

Accept it in the spirit it is given. Do not become defensive or argue with the person. Do not try to justify your position. Just listen. Ask questions for clarification. If you think the person is right, say so and thank them. If not, just thank them.

Job Performance Feedback: 7 Tips for Receiving Feedback Gracefully

1. *Welcome Constructive Feedback.* Your powers of self-perception only go so far. People around you notice things, both good and bad, which you may or may not see and you might learn from their input. There is a "virtuous circle" of feedback whereby the more you actively seek it out, the less you can hide bad behavior. EBay seller feedback is an excellent example of a transparent feedback process which encourages positive behaviors.

2. *Do Not Justify Your Position.* Telling the person why their feedback is wrong will not work. Arguing, justifying your

position, or denying anything is even wrong are all powerful negative emotions which make conversations more challenging than they need to be. The results from this type of behavior are usually hurt feelings and intense anger and distrust.

3. *Do Accept Feedback At Face Value.* Although the feedback might feel like a personal insult against you as a person, keep things in perspective. The feedback is usually about something specific that occurred which, now that you know about it, you can correct.

4. *Do Not Ruminate on Feedback.* Only cows need to ruminate before they digest. Chewing on, or thinking over and over again about feedback that is less than glowing will do nothing more than increase your feelings of resentment over receiving it. Avoid the temptation to re-enact the conversation with a friend as this only makes you feel ten times worse. Do talk about it with someone else, but make sure you are emotionally detached first.

5. *Do Evaluate Feedback Before Responding.* Feedback often tells you more about the person saying it than it does about you. For example, a person who says you never praise their work might have difficulty evaluating their work themselves. Teaching this person to do a good self-evaluation of their own performance might be a better approach than you trying to praise them over and over again. In the long run, you will be doing them a favor by giving them a much needed boost to their self-esteem.

6. *Do Not Throw Your Toys from the Pushchair.* Sulking, stonewalling or withdrawing from the person giving the feedback is childish. If need be, give yourself some space from the person, allowing yourself time to calm down and deal with the feedback and person as a rational adult.

7. *Do Make a Choice on How to Use the Feedback.* Feedback can be a gift allowing you to grow and develop as a person

in a job or in a relationship. On the other hand, some feedback is downright useless and best ignored. It is ultimately your choice how to act, or not, upon feedback received. For example, let's assume you receive internal customer feedback saying you do not do "x" and they think you should. You have actually spent some time considering "x" and have determined that it is simply not cost effective. Thank them for the feedback, letting them know the history of what you have done and then ask how else you could meet their needs. Chances are they will be satisfied with your explanation and not notice that you did not respond directly to their feedback.

Communicating Non-Defensively[4]

We are all naturally defensive to some degree, and it is no more apparent than in our communications with others.

What can lead us and others we work with towards defensive communications?

How do defensive communications interfere with problem solving and dealing with performance issues?

If we learn how to communicate non-defensively and teach others to do the same, we can:

- Reduce interpersonal conflict.
- Help people communicate more openly and honestly.

Five Skills to Communicating Non-Defensively:

1. Disengage
   - Back off from the situation
   - Take some time to think through the problem
   - Re-examine from a more objective viewpoint
   - Realize that it is probably not a personal attack

2. Empathize

- Imagine yourself in the other person's position
- Consider other viewpoints
- Let the other person know that you understand their perspective

3. Inquire

- Ask questions that allow you to learn more about the problem
- Get to the specifics of the issue
- Encourage both sides to focus on a solution, not the defensive problem
- Listen to all sides — use your active listening skills

4. Disclose

- Reveal your own needs and concerns in a non-defensive manner
- Be honest and direct
- Be attentive, but not overly apologetic
- Make "I" statements

5. Depersonalize

- Discuss the issue objectively
- See your work as what you do, not who you are
- As you change your behavior towards others, you shape their response to you

Why Might We Communicate Defensively?

- Low self-esteem — fear of being perceived as incompetent or fear of being criticized.
- Take the comments personally — assume the attack is personal rather than issue-based.

How Do People Respond to Defensive Communications?

- We shut down — fight back with passive aggression.

- We respond defensively, which creates a defensive chain and the cycle continues.

- The defensive chain can ripple out to others within the organization.

---

4   Adapted from *Communicating Non-Defensively, revised edition (1994).* Carlsbad, CA: CRM Learning, L.P.

Chapter 6

Project Management Leadership

Project Planning

Basic Project Planning and Management Steps

1. Analyze the project.

    *   Define the project

    *   List Project Objective Statement

    *   Should include criteria for project

    *   Major deliverables for project

    *   List the activities — develop Work Breakdown Structure

    *   Consider your workforce/resources

    *   Identify the time required for the activities

2. Determine a sequence for the project based on the activities involved, the workforce who will do the work, and the time required for the activities.

    *   Consider sequence-dependent activities (those tasks that must be done in sequence)

    *   Consider sequence-independent activities (tasks that can be done in parallel

3. Estimate resources needed for the project.

   - Consider your own internal resources
   - Obtain outside resources as required
   - Person doing the work must be the person estimating resources
   - Cannot estimate if you have no knowledge of how to do the job
   - Use efficiency factor: 6 work hours in an 8-hour day

4. Build a project management chart.

   - PERT or Gantt Chart or Critical Path Method
   - Synchronization Matrix
   - Important to determine critical path
   - Use Forward Pass/Backward Pass methods

5. Communicate the plan.

   - Your team, your supervisor, and your peers who may also be involved
   - Refine the plan as needed based on input
   - Use Network Communication Circle — free and open communications

6. Initiate the project.

   - Organize the team
   - Provide leadership for the project

7. Monitor progress.

   - Refine the plan and adjust as needed based on the evolving situation
   - Communicate updates as required to those who need to know

- Use effective decision-making during the project

- When conflict arises, remember smoothing, avoiding, forcing, compromising, collaboration response styles

  - Smoothing — focusing on the other person's view while minimizing real differences; used when things get emotional or when faced with time constraints

  - Avoiding — refusing to confront the conflict; used in hostile situations, when you have lack of authority to make decision, or when someone else can do it better

  - Forcing — using your power to resolve issue; used when you know decision is outside the project scope, when there is potential for legal issues, or when facing major time constraints

  - Compromise — willing to make concessions; used when you need their support, when it will not have major impact on project, when it is a no-win situation, or when you need something in return

  - Collaboration — willing to work together to resolve issue; used whenever possible unless you know it will create legal or ethical issues

  - Goal should be to collaborate whenever possible.

8. Complete the project.

   - Conduct an After Action Review (AAR). This is a process to review what worked and did not work by asking simple questions such as:

   1. What did we say we would do?

   2. Did we accomplish this?

   3. What worked well and what we should do again?

   4. What did not work well and we should discard in the future?

- Use the AAR results for continuous improvement in the workplace

- Determine Return on Investment (ROI) of project

- Use ROI Model:

A simple Return on Investment expresses the profitability of an investment in terms of a percentage of benefit on the original investment outlay.

Return on Investment = Net Benefit / Net Investment Cost x 100
In the ROI of data modeling, this would translate to:

Return on Investment = Net Savings Due to Data Modeling / Net Investment Cost in Data Modeling x 100

For example, assume a savings due to data modeling of $500,000, and a data modeling cost of $250,000. The return on investment is 200%.

ROI does not consider the time value of money or the economic life of the project. This is the most basic ROI model. Depending on your audience, you may want to consider more pertinent models.

Deliberate Decision-Making

The 7-Step Decision-Making Model

Step #1: Receive the Requirement

Requirements, tasks, missions, problems, ideas, questions, issues, etc., can come from anywhere. The challenge is to determine what you can readily solve and which ones require a deliberate decision-making process.

Step #2: Analyze the Requirement

- Describe and assess the operating environment. Possible considerations include the budget, existing plans, administrative requirements, environmental considerations, and any operational/logistical considerations.

- Identify facts and assumptions. A fact is what you know to be true. An assumption is what you think to be true, but need to verify before proceeding with the project.

- Identify specified and implied tasks. *Specified Task:* stated in the requirement, usually the operational tasks. *Implied Task:* not stated, but tasks you will need to accomplish in order to fulfill the requirement. Often implied tasks are the support (logistical/environmental) tasks associated with the requirement.

- Identify constraints. Constraints can take the form of a requirement to do something (for example, reduce costs by 10%) or a prohibition on action (for example, no increase in overtime).

- Determine essential tasks. Hilight the specified or implied tasks that are essential in order to fulfill the requirement.

Step #3: Re-State the Requirement

Re-write/re-phrase the requirement in terms of what you need to do. Include the essential tasks in the re-stated requirement. Include the "who/what/when/where/why" elements in the re-stated requirement.

Step #4: Develop Options

Develop 2 or 3 options. Options should be uniquely different from each other. Options are often based on the methods used to achieve the requirement (timeline, equipment involved, sequence of the operation, program management, etc.). Conduct a brain-storming session with your team. Good project managers will weigh options between both tasks and people. Failure to do so will usually result in bad decisions being made.

Step #5: Select the Best Option

Determine the best option and then make a recommendation. Use all the planning/decision making tools. Sometimes the best decision is to simply go with your "gut feel."

Explain your recommendation, providing a summary of your results and comparisons. When done, get the appropriate approval required to move forward.

Step #6: Implement the Best Option (A Written Plan)

- Situation. Describe the operating environment, your higher requirements, any additional assets available that are not normally assigned to your operation, and any non-validated assumptions.

- Re-state requirements. A concise statement of the project — who/what/when/where/why.

- Project Management. Project overview, project intent, project outcomes, sequence of operations/timetable, PERT/Critical Path Charts, and any contingencies, branches, sequels. Directed requirements/tasks (to your subordinate/adjacent units/departments).

- Logistical/Administrative Support. Includes Maintenance, Employee Relations/Safety, Contractors, Clerical, Permitting/Environmental, and any other support aspects to the project.

- Communications and Supervision. Includes flow of information, scheduled project updates, responsibilities of project manager, chain of command for the project.

Step #7: Lead, Monitor, and Refine the Decision

- Provide appropriate leadership for the successful accomplishment of the project (mentoring, teaching, coaching, directing, consensus building).

- Monitor the project (time tables/synchronization matrix, project management tools, forecasting).

- Prioritize your efforts (use critical events developed during option development).

- Refine the project by forecasting potential problems. ("If ___ occurs, then we shift the plan to ____"). Do not spend much time if you need to make minor changes; but use a change order or deliberate decision-making process if major changes are needed.

Use project management tools to help you prioritize and manage your work efforts.

Chapter 7

Stress Management for Leaders

Managing Stress

Stress is a natural occurrence for most people as they conduct their jobs. Learning to manage stress is a leadership skill that you need to master. Make no mistake: unmanaged stress can kill you or, at a minimum, shorten your life. The physical impacts of stress are real, relevant, and something you, as a leader, must be able to recognize.

Managing stress helps you to:

- Perform at the peak of your abilities when under immense pressure.

- Produce good quality work even when tasks are dull and repetitive.

- Improve the quality of your life, health and job.

- Avoid the problems of exhaustion, depression, ill health, burn-out, and breakdown that are associated with excessive levels of long term stress.

Consider stress to be anything that stimulates you and increases your level of alertness.

Life without stimulus would be incredibly dull and boring. Life with too much stimulus becomes unpleasant and tiring, and may ultimately damage your health or well-being. Too much stress can seriously interfere with your ability to perform effectively.

The art of stress management is to keep you at a level of stimulation that is healthy and enjoyable. Information provided here will help you to monitor and control stress so that you can find and operate at a level that is most comfortable for you. We will discuss strategies to reduce or eliminate sources of unpleasant stress. We will also explain what can happen when you do not control stress properly.

Most people realize that aspects of their work and lifestyle can cause stress. While this is true, it is also important to note that it can be caused by your environment and by the food and drink you consume. There are several major sources of stress:

- *Survival stress:* this may occur in cases where your survival or health is threatened, where you are put under pressure, or where you experience some unpleasant or challenging event. Here adrenaline is released in your body and you experience all the symptoms of your body preparing for "fight or flight."

- *Internally generated stress:* this can come from anxiously worrying about events beyond your control, from a tense, hurried approach to life, or from relationship problems caused by your own behavior. It can also come from an "addiction" to and enjoyment of stress.

- *Environmental and job stress:* here your living or working environment causes the stress. It may come from noise, crowds, pollution, untidiness, dirt or other distractions. Alternatively, stress can come from events at work.

- *Fatigue and overwork:* here stress builds up over a long period. This can occur when you try to achieve too much in too little time, or where you are not using effective time management strategies.

While a certain level of stress is necessary in order to avoid boredom, high levels of stress over a sustained period can damage your health. Note that as the stress you are under increases, your ability to recognize it often decreases.

The 50 Proven Stress Reducers

Consider these proven stress reducers for both personal and on-the-job stress relief.

1. Allow 15 minutes of extra time to get to appointments. Arrive at the airport at least 90 minutes before domestic departures.

2. Allow yourself time — every day — for privacy, quiet time, and thinking.

3. Always set up contingency plans — 'just in case.' ("If for some reason either of us is delayed, here is what we will do ... " kind of thing).

4. Ask questions. Taking a few moments to repeat directions or what you think someone wanted you to do can save hours.

5. Be flexible. Some things are worth not doing perfectly; some issues are best resolved with compromise.

6. Be optimistic. Most people are doing the best they can.

7. Be prepared to wait. A paperback, magazine, or e-book can make a wait in line almost pleasant.

8. Check your breathing throughout the day, especially before, during, and after high-pressure situations. If you find your stomach muscles are knotted and your breathing is shallow, relax all your muscles and take several deep, slow breaths. Note how, when you are relaxed, both your abdomen and chest expand when you breathe. When feeling stressed, most people breathe in short, shallow breaths. When this

occurs, stale air is not expelled, oxidation of the tissues is not complete, and the result is muscle tension.

9. Count your blessings. For every one thing that goes wrong there are probably 50 or 100 things that go right.

10. Do one thing at a time. When you are with someone, enjoy their company. When you are busy with a project, concentrate on doing that project and forget about everything else you have to do.

11. Do something for somebody else.

12. Do something that will improve your appearance. Looking better can help you feel better.

13. Do not forget to take a lunch break. Get away from your desk or work area in body and mind, even if it is just for 15 or 20 minutes.

14. Do not put up with something that does not work correctly. If your alarm clock, wallet, shoelaces, windshield wipers — whatever — are a constant source of aggravation, get them fixed or get new ones.

15. Do not rely on your memory. Write down appointment times, when to pick up the laundry, and when library books are due. ("The palest ink is better than the most retentive memory.")

16. Eliminate (or restrict) the caffeine and sugar in your diet.

17. Eliminate destructive self-talk: "I am too old to ... ," "I am too fat to ... ," etc.

18. Every day, do something you really enjoy. Example: Before speaking in public, visualize every part of the experience in your mind. Imagine what you will wear, what the audience will look like, how you will present your talk, and how you will answer questions. Visualize the experience the way you want it to turn out.

19. Focus on understanding rather than on being understood and loving rather than on being loved.

20. Forget about counting to 10. Count to 100 before doing something or saying anything that could make matters worse.

21. Get enough sleep. If necessary, use an alarm clock to remind you to go to bed.

22. Get up 15 minutes earlier in the morning. The inevitable morning mishaps will be less stressful.

23. Get up and stretch now and then if you have to sit for long periods in your job.

24. Have a forgiving view of things. Accept the fact that we live in an imperfect world.

25. If an "unpleasant" task faces you, do it early in the day and get it over with.

26. Inoculate yourself against a feared event. Just as vaccine containing a virus can protect you from illness, if you expose yourself to one or more of the dreaded aspects of an experience beforehand, you will probably feel less fearful.

27. Learn to delegate responsibility to others.

28. Learn to live one day at a time.

29. Make duplicates of all keys (label them!). Bury a house key in a secret spot in the garden; carry a duplicate car key in your wallet.

30. Make friends with non-worriers. Nothing can get you into the habit of worrying faster than association with a worrier.

31. Organize your home and workspace so that you always know exactly where things are. Put things away where they belong; you will not have the stress of trying to locate misplaced things.

32. Plan ahead. Do not let the gas tank get below one-quarter full; keep a well-stocked "emergency shelf" or home staples; do not wait until you are down to your last postage stamp to buy more.

33. Practice preventative maintenance. Your car, appliances, home, and relationships will be less likely to break down or fall apart "at the worst possible moment."

34. Prepare for the morning the evening before (e.g., set the breakfast table, make lunches, and lay out the clothes you plan to wear).

35. Relax your standards. The world will not end if the grass does not get mowed this weekend.

36. Say "no" to extra projects, social activities, and invitations you know you do not have time or energy for. This takes practice, self-respect, and a belief that everyone, every day needs quiet time to relax and be alone.

37. Schedule a fun day. Allow plenty of "breathing time" between appointments.

38. Select an environment (work, home, leisure) that matches your personal needs and desires. If you hate to talk politics, do not associate with people who live the subject.

39. Simplify, simplify, simplify.

40. Take a refreshing bath or shower to relieve tension.

41. Take care of today the best you can. The yesterdays and tomorrows will take care of themselves.

42. Talk it out. Discussing your problems with trusted friends can clear confusion.

43. Think "diversion." When stress gets in the way of getting a job done, take a break. Refresh yourself with a change in activity and/or environment.

44. Try the following yoga technique whenever you feel the need to relax. Inhale deeply through your nose to the count of eight. Then, with lips puckered, exhale very slowly though your mouth to the count of 16, or for as long as you can. Concentrate on the long sighing sound and feel the tension dissolve.

45. Turn "needs" into preferences. Our basic physical needs are food, water, and keeping dry and warm. Everything else is a preference. Do not get attached to preferences.

46. Turn off your phone if you want to take a bath, meditate, sleep, or read without interruption.

47. Use your weekend time for a change of pace. If your work week is slow and patterned, make sure there is action and time for spontaneity built into your weekends. If your work week is fast-paced and full of people and deadlines, seek peace and solitude during your days off.

48. Wear earplugs. If you need to find quiet, but Junior must practice the trombone, pop in some earplugs (available in any drugstore) — and smile.

49. Whatever you want to do tomorrow, do today; whatever you want to do today, do it now. Procrastination is stressful!

50. Write your thoughts and feelings down in a journal (or on paper to be thrown away). This will help you clarify things and give you a new perspective on things.

Planning to Manage Stress

We operate best at an optimum stress level. Not having enough stress leaves us feeling bored and lethargic. Having too much stress damages our performance in the short term, and can lead to unhappiness, exhaustion, burn-out and serious illness in the long term. It may not be obvious initially what causes you stress, whether you are effective in controlling it, or what your optimum stress level is.

Keeping a stress diary is an effective way of finding out both what causes your stress and what level of stress you prefer. In your diary, jot down your stress levels and how you feel throughout the day. In particular, jot down stressful events. After a few weeks you should be able to analyze this information. It may be interesting to note the outcomes of the jobs you were doing when you were under stress.

This should give you two types of information:

1. You should be able to understand the level of stress you are happiest with and the level of stress at which you work most effectively. You may find that your performance is good even when you feel upset by stress.

2. You should know what the main sources of unpleasant stress in your life are. You should understand what circumstances make stress particularly unpleasant, and you should begin to understand whether your strategies for handling the stress are effective or not.

It is probably only worth keeping the diary for a short period of time. You will find that the longer you keep the diary, the smaller the benefit of each additional day will be. If, however, your lifestyle changes or you begin to suffer from stress again in the future, it may be worth using the diary approach again. You will probably find that the stresses you face have changed. If this is the case, then keeping a diary again will help you to develop a different approach to dealing with them.

Once you understand the level of stress under which you work most effectively, and know precisely what is causing your stress, the next stage is to work out how to effectively manage the stress. The best way of doing this will probably be to make an action plan of things that you are going to do when stress occurs. Some elements of this action plan will be actions you are going to take to contain, control or eliminate problems that are causing you stress. Other elements may be health related such as exercising more, changing your diet, or improving the quality of your environment. Another part of the plan may be to develop stress management techniques that you will employ when stress levels begin to build.

Increasing Stress Levels — Psyching Up

When you are not feeling motivated about a task, either because you are bored by it or because you are tired, you may need to psych yourself up. This will increase your level of arousal so you can perform effectively.

You can use the following techniques to psyche up:

- Focus on the importance or urgency of the task.

- Set a challenge for yourself — i.e., to do the job in a particular time or to do it to a particularly high standard.

- Tell yourself — 'I can feel energy flowing into me'.

- Break jobs down into smaller jobs, doing each part between more enjoyable tasks. Take satisfaction from the successful completion of each element.

Stress Reduction Techniques

When choosing methods to combat stress, it is worth asking yourself where the stress comes from. If outside factors such as important events or relationship difficulties are causing stress, then a positive thinking- or imagery-based technique may be effective. When stress and fatigue are long term, lifestyle and organizational changes may be appropriate. If the feeling of stress comes from adrenaline in your body, it may help to relax the body and slow the flow of adrenaline. By anticipating stress you can prepare for it and work out how to control it when it happens. This can be carried out in a number of ways:

- *Rehearsal:* By running through a stressful event such as an interview or a speech several times in advance, you can polish your performance and build confidence.

- *Planning:* By analyzing the likely causes of stress, you will be able to plan your responses accordingly. This might include actions to alleviate the situation or may be stress management techniques that you will use. Regardless, it is important that you formally plan for this — it is of little use just worrying in an undisciplined way — this will be counter-productive.

- *Avoidance:* When a situation is likely to be unpleasant and will yield no benefit to you, avoid it. You should be certain in your own mind, however, that this is the case.

A number of factors can make an event take on a high level of significance and cause stress as a result:

- The importance and size of the event
- The prospect of a large financial reward, a promotion, or a personal advancement
- The presence of family, friends, or important guests.

If stress is a problem under these circumstances, then think carefully about the event — take every opportunity to reduce its importance in your eyes:

- If the event seems big, minimize it by comparing it in your mind to a bigger event you may have attended.
- If there is a financial reward, remind yourself that there may be other opportunities for reward later. Focus on the quality of your performance. Focusing on the rewards will only damage your concentration and raise stress.
- If members of your family are watching, remind yourself that they love you anyway. If friends are real friends, they will continue to like you whether you win or lose.
- If people who are important to your goals are watching, remind yourself that you may well have other chances to impress them. People who are supportive and want to see you succeed will give you the benefit of the doubt.

If you focus on correctly performing your tasks then the importance of the event will dwindle into the background.

Uncertainty can cause high levels of stress. Causes of uncertainty can be:

- Not having a clear idea of what the future holds:

    - Not knowing where your organization is going

    - Not having any career development plans

    - Not knowing what will be expected from you in the future

- Not knowing what your boss or colleagues think of your abilities.

- Receiving vague or inconsistent instructions.

In these cases, lack of information or the actions of other people are negatively affecting your ability to perform.

The most effective way of countering this is to ask for the information you need. This might include asking for information on your organization's performance. It may involve asking what your employer wants from you in the future so that you can set the appropriate career development goals. If you are unsure of how you are doing, ask for a performance review. When instructions are inconsistent or conflicting, ask for clarification. If you ask in a positive way, people are usually quite happy to help.

Thought Awareness, Rational Thinking and Positive Thinking

These three related tools are useful in combating negative thinking. Negative thinking causes stress because it damages your confidence that you are up to the task you face. Negative thoughts occur when you put yourself down, criticize yourself for errors, doubt your abilities, expect failure, etc. Negative thoughts also damage confidence, harms performance, and paralyzes mental skills.

Thought awareness is the process by which you observe your thoughts for a time, perhaps when under stress, and become aware of what is going through your head. It is best not to suppress any thoughts — just let them run their course while you observe them. Watch for negative thoughts while you observe your 'stream of consciousness'. Normally these appear and disappear unnoticed.

Examples of common negative thoughts are:

- Worrying about how you appear to other people.
- A preoccupation with the symptoms of stress.
- Dwelling on consequences of poor performance.
- Self-criticism; feelings of inadequacy.

Make a note of the thought and then let the stream of consciousness run on. Thought awareness is the first step in the process of eliminating negative thoughts — you cannot counter thoughts you do not know you think.

Once you are aware of your negative thoughts, write them down and review them rationally. See whether the thoughts have any basis in reality. Often you find that when you properly challenge negative thoughts they are obviously wrong. Often they persist only because they escape notice.

You may find it useful to counter negative thoughts with positive affirmations. You can use affirmations to build confidence and change negative behavior patterns into positive patterns. You can base affirmations on clear, rational assessments of fact, and use them to undo the damage that negative thinking may have done to your self-confidence.

Examples of affirmations are:

- I can do this.
- I can achieve my goals.
- I am completely at peace with myself and people will like me for myself.
- I am completely in control of my life.

- I learn from my mistakes. They increase the basis of experience on which I can draw.

- I am a well valued person in my own right.

Traditionally people have advocated positive thinking almost recklessly, as if it is a solution to everything. It should be used with common sense. No amount of positive thinking will make everyone who applies it an Olympic champion marathon runner (though an Olympic marathon runner is unlikely to have reached this level without being pretty good at positive thinking). Decide what goals you can realistically attain with hard work and then use positive thinking to reinforce these goals.

Physical relaxation techniques

These are useful when stress is caused by physical processes in your body; perhaps where muscles are tense, or where you are experiencing the effects of adrenaline. Exercising frequently is probably one of the best physical stress-reduction techniques available. Exercise not only improves your health and reduces stress caused by unfitness, but it also relaxes tense muscles and helps you to sleep.

Exercise has a number of other positive benefits you may not be aware of:

- It improves blood flow to your brain, increasing sugars and oxygen which may be needed when you are thinking intensely.

- When you think hard, the neurons of your brain function more intensely. As they do this they build up toxic waste products that cause decreased thinking in the short term and can damage the brain in the long term. By exercising, you speed the flow of blood through your brain, moving these waste products faster. You also improve this blood flow so that even when you are not exercising, waste is eliminated more efficiently.

- It can cause a release of chemicals called endorphins into your blood stream. These give you the feeling of happiness and well-being.

There are a lot of wrong approaches to exercise. Many traditionally recommended forms of exercise actually damage your body over the medium or long term. It is worth finding reputable and up-to-date sources of advice on exercise, possibly from a fitness specialist, and then having a customized exercise plan drawn up for you. An important thing to remember is that exercise should be fun — if you do not enjoy it, then you will probably not keep doing it.

Deep breathing is a very effective method of relaxation. It is the core component of everything including the 'take ten deep breaths' approach to calming someone down, as well as yoga relaxation and Zen meditation. It works well in conjunction with other relaxation techniques as Progressive Muscular Relaxation, relaxation imagery, and meditation to reduce stress.

Techniques for Reducing Long Term Stress

The main emphasis in the management of long term stress is on adjusting your working methods and your lifestyle. Formal relaxation techniques have a part in this, but equally important are time management skills, a positive attitude, a healthy diet with sufficient exercise and adequate rest, and a pleasant environment. Adjusting these things will improve the quality of your life as well as increase your resistance to stress.

Chapter 8

Leadership Ethics

Ethical Choices

Ethical leaders are fair, consistent, and place the interests of their organization and team above their own interests. Ethical leaders exemplify solid ethical conduct for their entire team, all the time.

Ethical leadership requires us to consider our organizational values along with our personal values as we conduct our business communications. Ethical leadership begins with identifying your own personal values and morals. You then need to know your organizational values or code of conduct. If your company does not have stated values or such a code, you should at least determine values and a code of conduct for your team.

Ethical decision-making requires us to consider more than just the decision itself. It requires us to consider the choices available in terms of our business ethics. You first need to recognize if a moral or ethical conflict exists, and then you have to evaluate alternatives from an ethical perspective in order to determine the right thing to do.

We frequently hear of an organization being accused of ethical misconduct. Almost all of these organizations had a code of ethics, detailed policies, and codes of conduct. But it is not the organization that behaved unethically. It was individuals who misbehaved for one reason or another. In most circumstances individuals themselves make ethical choices, right or wrong, not organizations.

Yet, in most cases, we are not talking about bad people. It is usually good people who make bad choices.

A Self-Assessment

Consider these questions for a few moments.

In the last six months have you or someone you know:

- Called in sick when you/they actually were not?
- Broken a confidence?
- Ignored a policy or procedure?
- Told a joke that might have offended someone?
- Covered up a mistake made by someone else?
- Covered up a mistake that you made?
- Used an organization's resources for personal use?
- Received too much change when making a purchase and kept the extra money?
- Made a copy of something without paying for it?
- Told a little white lie?
- Taken credit for someone else's efforts?
- Gossiped about someone in the office?
- Fudged on an expense report?
- Broke a "stupid" work rule?
- Reproduced some personal documents on a printer or copier at work?

The ultimate leadership responsibility is modeling the behaviors you expect from others. To a large degree, you operate in a fishbowl. Employees are constantly watching you and learning from you. They rightfully assume that it is okay to do whatever you do. Regardless of what is written or said elsewhere in the organization, your behavior is the performance standard employees will follow. That is a huge "comes with the territory" responsibility. But it is also a great opportunity to be able to influence the ethics of your work unit and the entire organization.

Who is responsible for acting ethically? You are! It is not the "company." It is not just the business owner. It is not only your manager. It is every person, regardless of position. Ultimately, each of us is responsible for our own actions, including being ethical. Considering the **"3R's"** will point you and your employees in the right ethical direction.

The first "R" of business ethics is **RESPECT**. It is an attitude that must be applied to people, organizational resources, and the environment. Respect includes behavior such as:

- Treating everyone (customers, co-workers, vendors, etc.) with dignity and courtesy.

- Using company supplies, equipment, time, and money appropriately, efficiently, and for business use only.

- Protecting and improving your work environment, and abiding by laws, rules and regulations that exist to protect our world and our way of life.

The second "R" of business ethics is **RESPONSIBILITY**. You have a responsibility to your customers, your co-workers, your organization and yourself. Included are behaviors such as:

- Providing timely, high-quality goods and services.

- Working collaboratively and carrying your share of the load.

- Meeting all performance expectations and adding value.

The third "R" of business ethics is **RESULTS**. Understanding that the way results are attained — the "means" — are every bit as important, if not more important, than the ultimate goals — the "ends." Using the phrase "The end justifies the means" is an excuse that is too often used to explain an emotional response or action that was not well planned or carefully considered.

Obviously, you are expected to get results for your organization and for your customers. However, you are also expected to get those results legally and morally, by being ethical. If you lose sight of this responsibility, you jeopardize your job, your business and your career.

Values-based Decision-Making

A values-based decision-making template

1. Discuss the situation and describe the difference between behavior observed and behavior expected based upon your mission, vision, and values.

2. Explore why there might be a difference between what is observed and what is expected.

3. Differentiate between the symptoms of the problem (what you are seeing) and the problem itself (why it might be occurring).

4. Develop a strategy to address the problem(s) with the person and/or others involved in the situation.

5. Identify specific conversational actions you will take and how you will use your mission, vision, and values to address the situation. What are your core messages?

As a leader, you have the ultimate responsibility for your actions. You, and you alone are responsible for the way you act. If you are a supervisor or manager, you need to provide the means that allow your people to act ethically. This is how an organization supports the ethical actions of its employees.

Knowing what is ethical and what is not is essential. However, far more difficult than knowing what is right is actually doing what is right. Doing the right thing is not always easy, but it is always right. It is a requirement for long-term success.

The first step in doing what is right is to ask yourself if it meets ethical or moral guidelines before moving ahead or implementing a decision.

Use the questions below for guidance to test if a decision or action is ethical or moral. These are similar to the guidelines for knowing what is right.

If you answer "no" to any one of the questions, you should develop an alternate strategy or seek counsel and advice from appropriate sources.

Doing what is right: Ethical action test for ideas and actions:

- Is it legal?
- Does it comply with company rules and regulations?
- Is it in sync with organizational values?
- Will you be comfortable and guilt-free if you do it?
- Is it in line with stated commitments and guarantees?
- Would I do it to my family or friends?
- Would it be okay for someone to do it to me?
- Would the most ethical person you know do it?
- How would this look on the front page of my local newspaper?

These are very practical and useful tests of your ideas and actions which will help you live up to your responsibility to be ethical and successful. However, you should not limit these to only your business dealings. Remember, acting ethically is not something you simply turn on and turn off. It is a part of everything you do.

When In Doubt About Ethics Questions — ASK!

There is a common phrase in today's business world that people use to justify their actions or determine ways to overcome the obstacles of bureaucracy, "red tape," and move a project ahead. This phrase is: *It is easier to ask for forgiveness than to ask for permission.*

In the context of ethics, however, this statement is incorrect and could actually cause people to act unethically. When dealing with ethics, this concept would serve you best if you reversed it: *It is better to ask for permission than to ask for forgiveness.*

The reason for this is that the stakes in behaving ethically in business are very high. We see weekly, if not daily, reports in the news media of how one or two people made poor ethical choices that caused disaster in their company. One poor decision could potentially impact hundreds, even thousands of people. When the results of the decisions you make have the potential to impact so many, it is better to ask for permission before you act.

You are expected to continually do what is right and ethical at work. There are resources available to you (e.g. employee handbook, the organization's mission, vision, and values; the values and attributes of leadership; etc.) to help meet that expectation. Use those resources when needed and obtain input from others whenever you can.

Whenever you are unsure if an action you are about to take is appropriate or not, ask a proper authority such as your boss, a senior manager, a mentor, the owner (if you work at a small company), someone in the Human Resources Department, or in the Legal Department for counseling. The most important thing to remember is to keep asking until you get an answer.

Business Ethics and Compliance

Business ethics involves a lot more than compliance with company policies, laws, and financial regulations. Most organizations do not have problems with people following these rules and regulations. Instead, it is the "little things" that cause problems. It is our day-to-day seemingly insignificant actions and behaviors that have the greatest chance of causing ethical issues.

The little things that we do every day can become so repetitious that we tend to forget we are even doing them. However, the "little things" we do can have a significant impact on people who observe these behaviors. Remember, your behavior sets an example. Even if you are not the boss, there is always someone watching you for cues on how to act in certain situations — whether good or bad. These observers may be your fellow workers, neighbors, your spouse, or your children. What messages are you "sending" by your actions, words and attitudes?

To help you examine your personal ethics and see where you stand and where you need to improve, consider the following:

- "Little white lies" you tell
- Jokes you share
- The way you treat and talk about co-workers
- Things you say and do to make a sale
- E-mails you write and those you forward
- The way you handle customer complaints (including the number of people they get passed to)
- What you put on your billing sheets, time sheets, and expense reports
- Office supplies you take home
- Commitments you do not keep
- Personal business you conduct at work
- "Unimportant" work rules you fail to follow

- Non-work items you reproduce on the copy machine
- Standards you set for yourself
- The level of quality you put into whatever you do
- Credit you share with others

These and scores of additional behaviors like them, reflect who you are and what you stand for. When it comes to ethics and integrity, everything is important — including (and especially) "the small stuff."

Know What Cannot Be Compromised

Every business owner knows that there are some aspects of work that are discretionary and other aspects that must be followed exactly.

Discretionary areas of business are those situations where you and your employees have room to maneuver, compromise, bargain, and make deals as long as they are within certain pre-established boundaries.

Non-discretionary areas are topics or situations with very specific rules and regulations that must be followed exactly as written and expected. Compromise or deviation are unacceptable in these areas.

Safety is one non-discretionary area that immediately comes to mind. There are certain safety procedures that MUST be followed according to very specific guidelines. Any exceptions to the rules could pose danger to workers. However, there are other areas where your employees may not have quite as clear of an understanding of what is ethically correct and what is not.

To act ethically, it is vitally important that you, as a leader, understand what actions fall into each of these two areas — discretionary or non-discretionary. It is also important that you pass this understanding on to all team members as well as everyone else within the organization.

Different organizations and businesses provide different guidelines on operational latitude. These differences may be due to the responsibilities that employees have in performing certain jobs. Or, the job requirements themselves may permit only a certain procedure.

Universal Norms

However, there are several areas where zero tolerance for violations is allowed regardless of the organization. These universally accepted norms include:

- Laws and regulations
- Public and employee safety
- Truthfulness and accuracy of records and statements.

Stop and think what would happen if you did not obey laws and regulations. In addition, most safety rules were created because injuries occurred or obvious danger existed in workplaces. Finally, business is based on trust and truthfulness. If records and statements are not accurate, trust is lost.

Company Specific Standards

Businesses may add specific policies and procedures they wish to enforce for the well-being of the company or to simply differentiate their company from competitors. In all cases, ethics simply cannot be compromised. As a leader, you must set the example to ensure that team members know what the ethical boundaries are.

As a leader, you may be faced with a situation where an employee proposes an action or solution that you believe is not ethical or is outright wrong. What do you do? What do you tell the employee?

You may be tempted to do what is asked because you know the person or you feel obligated for some other reason. In any event, fight the temptation. Take a stand and say "NO," but say it with tact and respect.

Do not accuse the other person of being unethical. Instead, use "I" statements to describe your feelings. State your objection and concern without "indicting" them.

Here is how:

- *I have serious concerns about that, and I need your understanding ...*

- *I honestly believe it is wrong because ...*

- *I cannot do what I feel is wrong ...*

Propose an alternate action that you feel is ethical.

- *I think I know what you want to accomplish, and I feel there is a better way to do it. How about ...*

Ask for the person's help and agreement.

- *I really need your help.*

- *I want to make sure we both do the right thing.*

- *Will you go along with me on this one?*

Here are some words of wisdom from well-known individuals about this topic:

"Keep true, never be ashamed of doing right, decide on what you think is right, and stick to it." — George Elliot

"If you do not stand for something, you will fall for anything." — Multiple sources.

"To know what is right and not do it is the worst cowardice." — Confucius.

"Honesty is the cornerstone of all success, without which confidence and ability to perform cease to exist." — Mary Kay Ash.

"It is not who is right, but what is right, that is of importance." — Thomas H. Huxley.

Acting ethically sets an example. Others see your actions. Once the ethical barrier has been breached, others may assume it is appropriate to act unethically and improperly in any situation.

Knowing What is Ethical Takes On More Importance As Business Scandals Make Headlines

Investigations of many high-profile companies accused of unethical conduct show that most had elaborate policies or guidelines on ethics. The company did not break the rules. Instead, it was one or more individuals who did not follow the established policies and guidelines. Again, regardless of the code of ethics put into place, a key point to remember is that organizations do not make ethical decisions. Individuals do. A business or organization simply provides the environment for people to act ethically and morally.

To help you determine if your actions are ethical, compare them to these six basic guidelines for ethical business operations.

1) **Laws:** Laws are created to help society function. Is the action you are considering legal? Do you know the laws governing the activity? In general, ignorance of a law is no excuse for breaking the law.

2) **Rules and Procedures**: Companies create specific policies and procedures to help ensure success of the business and to avoid problems. How does your planned action compare to what is stated in the company's policies and procedures?

3) **Values:** These social principles help to create society's laws and a company's policies and procedures. In turn,

laws and policies reinforce the values. One example of values is to ask yourself: "Does the action I am considering follow not only the letter of the law, but also the 'spirit' of the law?" Is your action in agreement with the overall purpose of a law or rule? Or are you attempting to find a loophole?

4) **Conscience:** This internal sense of right and wrong develops at an early age. Your conscience recognizes certain principles that lead to feelings of guilt if you violate the principles. Will your actions make you feel guilty? Can you truly justify your actions to yourself?

5) **Promises:** Business is based upon trust. It is the belief that you will deliver on what you say you will do. Will your action live up to the commitment that you made to the other person (customer, client, supplier, employee, and employer) in the business relationship? Will your action build more trust?

6) **Heroes:** Every person has at least one individual who is a role model in some way. A hero may be a parent, teacher, coach, mentor or friend. Is your action something that your hero would do in the same situation? How would your hero act?

Using these six guidelines, along with the other information contained within this section, will help you in your decision making and ensure that your actions are legal, ethical, and according to your organization's standards and procedures.

Chapter 9

Time Management and Delegation

Time Management

Perhaps one of the biggest challenges you will have as a leader is to manage your time effectively. You will be pulled in several directions on a daily basis, typically all at the same time. Between the office requirements, your team needs, and the organizational demands, you will be hard pressed to try to get everything done.

Effective time management skills can help you deal with the day-to-day demands and help lower stress which is an important supervisory consideration as you make your leadership transition. In this section we will discuss what time management means and offer several practical tools that can help you to better manage your time and perhaps, even manage your life.

Prioritization

Prioritization is an essential task needed to make the best use out of your team's efforts.

It is more important when time is limited and demands are unlimited.

With good prioritization, you can bring order to chaos, reduce stress, and successfully complete essential tasks.

Prioritization based on project-value or profitability is the most commonly used.

Time constraints are important when other people are depending on you to complete a task.

Pressure from other sources to complete a job generally takes prioritization over other tasks.

General Tips and Techniques for Improving Your Time Management

- Clear your desk and plan your activities for the next day.

- First, list your time specific items, e.g. meetings, and then write down the tasks you have to complete.

- Once you have prioritized your tasks, make a "to do" list and work through the items in order of priority.

- Ensure that you have given yourself sufficient time to complete your "to do" list, taking into account your daily interruptions.

- Complete difficult jobs first, when you are at your best. Attend to minor jobs when you are tired.

- Set deadlines for all jobs and stick to them. A task should only take the time set aside for it.

- Do not postpone important matters that are unpleasant. Jobs rarely get more pleasant by being postponed. Do them now!

- Try to arrange set times for routine jobs such as going through the mail, talking with your manager or staff, computer input, etc.

- Try to set up times when you are not to be disturbed for anything other than emergency purposes.

- Plan your telephone calls. Make a brief note of what you want to say and what you want to find out. It saves time later.

- If you have several phone calls to make, make them all in the same pre-allotted timeframe.

- When you start a job, try to finish it without interruptions. If you have to finish it later, you will lose time picking up where you left off.

- Arrange your breaks at times when you cannot work effectively.

- Plan some time for discussing routine matters with your colleagues. Then you avoid interrupting each other all the time.

- Learn to say "No." Get used to asking yourself, "Am I the right person for this job?"

- Monitor how you use your time and make conscious changes to your behavior.

- Stress and fatigue are rarely caused by the things you have done, but by the thought of what you have not done!

- Make it a habit to finish the most important job of the day before you go home.

How planning helps you to use your time effectively

Planning can be considered an investment in efficiency and success. Planning is the process by which you work out what you want to achieve, and then think through "who, what, when, where, why and how" of achieving that goal in the most effective way possible.

Planning can help ensure that you focus your time and efforts on tasks critical to your goals instead of on tasks that have little to no effect on the overall desired outcomes.

Planning can be broken down into two main categories: *personal planning*, which is best done by setting goals, and *project planning*, which is best achieved by a formalized application of the planning process.

Goal setting is a formal process of setting personal targets in a number of areas. The process of setting goals on a routine basis helps you decide what you want to achieve with your time and then establish precise personal strategies for achieving this.

Setting goals has the additional benefit of raising your self-confidence by allowing you to recognize your ability and competence when you achieve your goal.

To Do lists are simply a way of organizing your day effectively by ranking tasks in order of importance. They are lists of tasks relevant to the daily goals which could encompass very specific targets you have for the day or simply the efficient use of your time for the day.

Even though To Do Lists are very simple by nature, they can be extremely powerful when used to organize your day which in itself will help reduce your levels of stress.

Problems can often seem too large or you may simply feel overloaded with the number of demands on your time. This can leave you feeling hopeless and lost. The solution is often as simple as writing each task down and then breaking it into smaller sub-tasks. If still too large, break it down again. Then prioritize all of the tasks and sub-tasks by order of importance. By doing this, it will allow you to separate those 'truly important' jobs from those 'trivial' everyday tasks, thereby giving you more control over your day and reducing stress.

Delegation

Delegation involves passing responsibility for the completion of work to other people. This section examines the reasons why you should delegate, how to delegate, what happens when you fail to delegate, and what should not be delegated. Delegation is useful for the following reasons:

- Once people have learned how to work with you, and learned what you do, they can take responsibility for jobs you do not have time to do.

- It allows you to develop people to look after routine tasks that are not cost-effective for you to do.

- It transfers work to people whose skills in a particular area may very well be better than yours, thereby saving time and unnecessary effort.

- Transferring responsibility develops your staff and can increase their job satisfaction.

Your goal as a manager should be to let your staff carry out those routine activities that normally take up most of your day. This will leave you time to do those more important tasks critical to the success of your organization.

How to Delegate

The following points may help you in delegating jobs:

- *Deciding what to delegate*: One way of deciding what to delegate is to create a list of everything that you do. Then rate each item according to the order of importance, the time it takes to accomplish each, and the return on investment for your time. Those tasks ranked the lowest in each category should then become the items that you begin to delegate.

- *Select capable, willing people to carry out jobs*: How far down the line you delegate jobs will depend on the ability, experience and reliability of your people. Good people will be able to carry out large jobs with no intervention needed. Inexperienced or unreliable people will need close supervision, coaching, and mentoring to help improve their abilities to carry out larger and more important tasks in the future.

- *Delegate complete jobs*: It is much more satisfying to work on a task as a whole than to simply be delegated fragments of the task. This helps ensure completeness of the job as well as continued pride and responsibility on the part of the person to whom you delegated the task.

- *Explain why the job is important and what the expected outcomes are*: When you delegate a job, explain how it fits into the overall picture of what you are trying to achieve. Ensure that you effectively communicate:

  ¤ The importance of the job

  ¤ The results that are expected

  ¤ The constraints within which the job must be performed

  ¤ The deadlines for completion

  ¤ Dates when you want progress updates

- *Then let go:* Once you have decided to delegate a task, let the person you delegated the task to get on with it. Check in with them periodically, but do not constantly look over their shoulders. Recognize and accept the fact that they may know a better way of doing something than you do. If they make a mistake, that is okay as long as it was not because of poor work practices or simply not doing the job. Mistakes are a great way for them to learn and grow.

- *Help and coach when requested:* It is important to support your subordinates when they are having difficulties, but do not do the job for them. If you do, then they will not develop the confidence to do the job themselves. Simply offer suggestions when they come to you seeking help.

- *Accept only finished work:* You have delegated a task in order to take things off your plate. Accepting partially completed jobs will do nothing more than fill your plate again and deny the persons to whom you delegated the task the experience they needed to complete the task to the end.

- *Give credit when a job has been successfully completed:* Public recognition builds the pride and confidence of the person who carried out the task and sets a standard for other employees to follow.

Despite the many advantages of delegation, some leaders do not delegate. This can be for the following reasons:

- *Lack of time:* Delegating jobs takes time. Initially, you will need to invest time in training people to do the tasks you are delegating to them. You will also have to devote time to check on them, monitor their progress, and answer any questions they may have. Ultimately, until they learn how to do the task, it will probably take longer than if you completed the task yourself. However, over time you will realize a return on the investment of your time when a well trained staff is able to help out when needed.

- *Perfectionism — fear of mistakes:* Just as you have to develop staff to do jobs without your involvement, you will have to let people make mistakes, and then help them to correct them. Most people will, with time, learn to do jobs correctly.

- *Enjoying 'getting hands dirty':* By doing jobs yourself you will probably get them done efficiently. But if doing this job takes work away from your team or takes you away from more important things that you should be doing, then your entire department will suffer. In addition, you will be sending the message that you do not trust them to do anything.

- *Fear of surrendering authority:* Whenever you delegate, you surrender some element of authority (but not of responsibility!) This is inevitable. By effectively delegating, however, you get the benefits of having adequate time to do YOUR job really well.

- *Fear of becoming invisible:* When your department is running smoothly, it may appear that you have nothing to do. This is the time for you to think, plan, and improve your department's process (and possibly even plan your next career move).

- *Belief that staff 'are not up to the job':* Good people will often under-perform if they are bored. Delegation will often bring the best out in them. People who are not so good will not be effective unless you invest time in them. Even seemingly incompetent people can be effective provided they find their niche. The only people who truly cannot be delegated to are those with super inflated egos of themselves.

It is common for people who are newly promoted to managerial positions to have difficulty delegating. They have often been promoted because they were good at what they were doing in their old job. The temptation then is for them to continue doing their old job instead of trying to learn their new job. This robs their subordinates of the opportunity to learn new tasks and grow their own careers, so avoid this at all costs.

While you should delegate as many tasks as possible, especially those that are not cost effective for you to carry out, ensure that you do not delegate control of your team. Remember that you bear the ultimate responsibility for the success or failure of your team.

Steps in Delegation

Introduce the task

Demonstrate clearly what needs to be done

Ensure understanding

Allocate authority, information, and resources

Let go

Support and monitor

Introduce the Task

1. Determine tasks to be delegated

   - Those tasks you completed prior to assuming your new role

   - Those tasks your delegatees have more experience with

   - Routine activities

   - Those tasks outside the scope of your expertise

2. Determine tasks to retain

   - Supervision of subordinates

   - Long-term planning

   - Tasks only you can do

   - Assurance of program compliance

   - Dismissal of employees, performance counseling, etc.

3. Select the delegatee

   - Look at individual strengths and weaknesses

   - Determine interest areas

   - Determine need for development of delegate

Demonstrate Clearly

1. Show examples of previous work

2. Explain objectives

3. Discuss timetable, set deadlines

Ensure Understanding

1. Clear communications

2. Ask for clarification

3. Secure commitment

4. Do not say no to them

5. Collaboratively determine methods for follow-up

Allocate ... Authority, Information, Resources

1. Grant authority to determine process, not desired outcomes

2. Provide access to all information sources

3. Refer delegatee to contact all individuals or specific resources that have assisted previously

4. Provide appropriate training to ensure success

Let go ...

1. Communicate delegatee's authority

2. Step back, let them work

3. Use constrained access

4. Do not allow for reverse delegation

Support and Monitor

1. Schedule follow-up meetings

2. Review progress

3. Assist, when requested

4. Avoid interference

5. Publicly praise progress and completion

6. Encourage problem solving

Delegation Stressors

#1 Loss of control? *If you train your subordinates to do a task the same way you would yourself, then they will be exercising your control on your behalf.*

#2 Too much time spent on explaining tasks? *The amount of time spent up front can be burdensome. But, continued use of delegation may free you up to complete other tasks and/or gain you some time for yourself to plan and think ahead.*

#3 Compromising your own value? *By successfully utilizing appropriate delegation, your value to the group/organization will grow at a greater rate as you will have more time to do more of the key leadership things.*

Consequences of Poor Delegating

- Information and decision-making not shared by the group

- Leaders burn out

- When leaders leave groups, no one has experience to carry on

- Group morale becomes low and people become frustrated and feel powerless

- The knowledge and skills of the group/organization are shared by only a few people

- New members do not find ways to contribute to the work of the group.

Chapter 10

Leading Change

Why Change?

Whether you are talking about re-engineering your business, restructuring your organization, promoting cultural transformation, or keeping pace with your industry, you are talking about change. As you go through change processes you will gain an understanding of why change initiatives fail and you will become familiar with the specific challenges of change.

There are three specific stages of change leadership: establishing a sense of urgency, putting together the change coalition, and developing the change vision. As you master these skills as a leader, you will have a clear idea of what it takes to initiate the change process in a manner that ensures success.

Change is inevitable and the rate at which we as a society have been changing has grabbed headlines for many years. Nations around the world are experiencing dramatic shifts in their political, economic and social structures.

Even in our daily lives, we are being inundated with information from the news media, advertising, and the World Wide Web.

The amount of information available to us in today's society is staggering. This has led some to believe that we have now moved from the Information Age to the Knowledge Age. They go on to say that because of the fact that we are so immersed with information, there is a great need to figure out an effective way to filter that information that has value from that which is meaningless.

The defining characteristic of the Knowledge Age is perpetual change. Unlike previous transformations, the move to the Knowledge Age is not a period of change followed by stability. It comes packaged with an epoch of continuous change on an accelerating time cycle. This means that the kinds of knowledge that will serve individuals and our society as a whole are constantly evolving.

Consider these facts: One of the key skills of effective leaders is the ability to create and lead change. When change is completed effectively, the organization adapts, learns, and achieves its goals. However, all too often change efforts fail as they are met with resistance and fear. Change can be as minor as relocating to a different office or as major as rapid growth or downsizing.

These tips and tools will help you prepare for and lead effective change.

1. *Create a clear vision.* Define where you want to be. Do the necessary work to fully commit to the change.

2. *Build a case for change.* State where you are now versus where you need to be. Build a compelling case as to why there exists the need for change. Change causes stress and discomfort because of the unknowns that come with it. Build excitement, commitment, and awareness of the need for change. Then gather support and gain agreement for your vision of the future.

3. *Build a powerful guiding coalition.* Identify those people important to helping gain commitment for the change. As a team, brainstorm ideas and formulate strategies on how

you will overcome barriers to the change. Plan out those steps necessary to transition through the period of change.

4. *Clarify roles.* Make sure that each person fully understands their role in the change process and feels appreciated for their contribution.

5. *Make sure you have the right players.* Select those people who are open to change. Support them with the training and resources that are needed.

6. *Encourage constant open communication.* Communicate your progress to the organization as well as what the next steps are on a regular basis. Feedback needs to occur at all levels: up, down, and laterally.

7. *Encourage risk taking and brainstorming.* Respect differences and test out new ideas and methods. Keep what works and get rid of what does not.

8. *Sustain your belief in the change effort.* Believe in the change effort and communicate that belief through your actions and words.

9. *Be prepared for the normal emotional reactions to change.* Change can create instability, anxiety, conflict, and fear of the unknown. Lead people through this field of emotions by expressing empathy and using flexible leadership tactics.

10. *Celebrate success.* Acknowledge short term gains and communicate to the others the successful change efforts.

Resistance to Change

10 Good Reasons Why People Resist Change and the Strategies to Overcome the Resistance[5]

1. *Surprise:* People often resist change because they have had little time to mentally prepare for the change.

   • Do not wait until all the decisions have been made before announcing them to an unsuspecting work group.

- Give advance notice and build commitment from the beginning.
- Include employees in the planning phase.
- Prepare and disseminate the vision as early as you can.

2. *Self-Doubt:* When faced with change, people often ask "Can I do this?", "Do I have the skills?", "Will I have to start all over again?" Feelings of inadequacy can undermine self-confidence which can lead to people holding on to that which is familiar.

- Provide additional training to employees.
- Provide opportunities to practice new skills.
- Maintain an open environment for asking questions and receiving feedback.

3. *Loss of Control:* When people feel they have no power over decisions that affect them, they may become over-controlling in order to grasp something they can control — their refusal to adapt to the change.

- When practical, provide the opportunity for the employees to make choices.
- Involve employees in the change process from the start.
- Provide a continuous flow of information — do not wait until the end.

4. *Debilitating Uncertainty:* Uncertainty about what changes will bring is an inherent part of the change process. When uncertainty becomes overwhelming, it can cause too much discomfort — it can become too dangerous to allow for the possibility of change.

- Form a clear and concise vision.
- Build milestones into the schedule.
- Leaders must set the example by taking the first steps themselves.

5. *Disruption of Routines:* With change, known routines and habits are thrown into turmoil which can cause people to possibly make mistakes on tasks that were previously performed effortlessly and error-free.

- Do not change what does not need to change.
- Have and publish a change management plan.
- Maintain familiar work surroundings.
- Avoid wild changes that simply symbolize the new way.

6. *Loss of Face:* People often infer that accepting changes means accepting that the way things were done in the past was wrong. To avoid looking stupid, people may feel they have to defend the old system. Unfortunately, leaders often try to sell changes by pointing out the failures of the old methods.

- Listen to the concerns.
- Do not sell the change by making the old system look bad. Simply make the new approach look better.
- Use employee experience and knowledge to develop new and better methods — build upon past success.

7. *Increased Workload:* Change often requires more energy, more time — simply more work! The extra work alone can be a cause of resistance.

- Communicate with families if extra work time is involved.
- Give credit and recognition if additional work time is required.
- Establish a reward system for the contributions, not just the additional time.
- Make certain that expectations match capabilities.
- Provide additional resources when needed.

8. *Dangers are Real:* Some change may create winners and losers — sometimes people will lose status or even their

jobs as a result of the change. People often ask "how will this change affect me?" and the answer may very well be negative.

- Leaders must be candid and open regarding the dangers associated with the change.

- Do not make false promises.

- If some will be negatively affected, let them know as soon as you can.

- Bad news does not get better with age.

9. *Institutional Memory:* Past negative experience with similar changes or unresolved issues can fuel resistance. People may ask "Have we not done this (unsuccessfully) before?"

- Listen to your employees, both as individuals and in groups.

- Empathize with differing viewpoints.

- Provide "outs" for those unwilling/unable to cope with the new change (e.g. layoff packages, early retirements, transfers, etc.).

10. *Personal Disruption:* Resistance to change may be the result of things that are not job-related. Changes in the workplace can disrupt family routines or personal plans; people may resist in order to maintain order outside of the workplace.

- Leaders must be sensitive to disruptions caused by the change initiative.

- Develop ways to meet those employee needs previously satisfied by the old ways.

- Work with employee schedules.

- Allow some "grieving" time for the loss of the past.

Eight Common Errors Associated with Change Initiatives

1. Not establishing a great enough sense of urgency.
2. Not creating a powerful enough guiding coalition.
3. Lack of vision.
4. Under-communicating the vision.
5. Not removing obstacles to the new vision.
6. Not systematically planning for and creating short term wins.
7. Declaring victory too soon.
8. Not anchoring changes in the organization's culture.

Sustaining Change

Promote a sense of curiosity within the organization. Never be satisfied with the current level of organizational knowledge.

Look and listen for current trends and knowledge. Keep your vision focused forward. Do not use team concepts to make everyone a generalist.

Build on unique skills and encourage learning across the board. Allow people to take a "try it and learn" approach.

Leaders must look beyond today and reach for tomorrow. By focusing too much effort on today's customers and their needs, future customers will go unheard and opportunities will be lost.

Look for meta-routines by asking the questions "Why are we doing this? Why are we doing it this way?" Leadership is essential in order to build, nurture, and sustain core capabilities.

Barriers to Effective Change

The Six Barriers to Change

1. *No compelling case for change:*

- Failing to "paint the right picture" of the future state
- Poor employee involvement and discussion
- Failing to build up the case for change over time — too rushed
- Failing to share key data with employees — lack of transparency

2. *Not understanding what change is*:
   - Failing to see change as a journey, not a single event
   - Over-simplified view of "getting the change out the way"

3. *Little or no employee involvement:*
   - Failing to involve employees in feedback sessions
   - Failing to involve employee teams in optimizing solutions and developing implementation plans that will work

4. *Ownership confusion:*
   - Failing to clearly establish who is responsible for what and who is making the decisions

5. *Ineffective implementation:*
   - Viewing implementation as the "easy part"
   - Failing to clarify who is coordinating implemen-tation
   - An unclear transition plan of roles and responsibilities
   - Poor alignment of the senior team around leadership behaviors
   - Poor communication — confusion about what is happening, and when

6. *Perpetuating "the way we do things here" too long:*
   - Failing to see the impact of the wider sector or economic environment

- "Good times" may have masked some less than effective management practices

Leading Change

Step #1: Establish a sense of urgency

- Overcome complacency. A compelling need has to be developed and shared. Visible crises catch peoples' attention and drive up the urgency levels.

- A clear case for change, approved at the appropriate level.

- The right climate for change — lay the ground work with stakeholders to create an initial sense of involvement and engagement with the challenge.

- An understanding of the timescale involved, even if it is not fully defined.

- An understanding of the consequences of not changing.

Step #2: Create a guiding coalition

- Power and credibility: To legitimize change (critical mass), ability to reward/confront.

- Pain and sacrifice: Personal stake. Pursue change despite personal needs.

- Expertise: Informed and intelligent decision making.

- Public/private role: Commitment and ability to support change publicly/meet privately with agents.

- Pitfalls: Avoid those who create mistrust or put their own immediate interests above the greater goal.

- Who is accountable and approves changes?

- Who is responsible as leader of the change process?

- How will stakeholders be involved?
- Clarify the difference between line responsibility and support.
- R.A.C.I.
  - □ Who is *Responsible*? What are they responsible for?
  - □ Who is *Accountable*? Do people understand this?
  - □ Who will be *Consulted* (before decisions are made)?
  - □ Who will be *Informed* (after decisions are made)?
- Identifying and involving "change champions."

Step #3: Develop a vision and strategy

Vision: Develop, articulate, and communicate a shared vision of the desired change that is:

- Imaginable — Creates a Picture
- Desirable — Appeals to the long-term interest
- Feasible — Realistic and Attainable
- Focused — Clearly guides decisions
- Flexible — Allows for changing conditions
- Communicable — Successfully explained in 5 minutes.

Step #4: Communicate the vision

- Keep it simple. Lose the jargon. Create "verbal" pictures.
- Lead by example. Your behavior speaks loudly and clearly.
- 2-Way: Listen and share. Recognize that everything you say and do is part of the communication process.
- Develop a communication plan that includes how and when you will tell people what, and by which medium. Be as open as you can and tell the truth — even if this means saying you do not know or cannot say

- Communicate on a regular basis, even if there is little to say. It is much more important to "keep the regular channels open" than to "only say what you need to say when you need to say it." Seek feedback at every opportunity to encourage involvement.

- It is important to build and maintain a project plan for any change project. Include major tasks, deliverables, timeline, who does what, risk assessment, logistical issues, etc. A general project planning process is critical.

Step #5: Empower Employees

- Senior managers are the driving force and must walk the talk.

- Deploy the vision and motivate the masses.

- Target resistance, measure readiness, and assess existing people/structures.

- Develop, train, reinforce, and support.

- Create a culture of empowerment, trust, and support.

- Set up measurement processes with clear targets.

- Focus on dealing with problems and potential roadblocks.

Step #6: Generate short-term wins

- Plan for and create regular "wins."

- Recognize and reward people who facilitate the "wins."

- When momentum builds resistance declines.

Step #7: Consolidate Gains

- Use increased credibility to change other systems that do not fit the vision.

- Hire, promote, and develop people who implement the change vision.

- Reinvigorate the process with new projects, themes, and change agents.

Step #8: Anchor new approaches

- May involve turnover.
- Maintain clear focus.
- Cultural change comes last, not first.
- Embrace and overcome the resistance.
- Respect those who resist.
- Continual reinforcement of the shared vision.
- Reinforce behaviors in others.
- Recognize and take the "best of the past" with us.
- Celebrate victories as a team.
- Create realistic yet challenging goals and objectives.
- Maintain a strong sense of "we will succeed or fail together."

---

5   Adapted from James O.B. Keener's 1999 booklet, *10 Good Reasons Why People Resist Change: And Practical Strategies that Win the Day.* Grand River, IW: Grand River Pub.

Chapter 11

Performance Management

Identifying and Solving Performance Problems

Managing performance on a day-to-day basis is essential in order to provide your team the leadership that motivates, inspires, and cultivates high quality performance. Conflicts and problems are common to most teams. Effectively dealing with these issues through problem solving, corrective action, and performance counseling will help you achieve the most from your team and subordinates.

Discipline is a condition that exists when employees follow or fail to follow established policies and procedures. Employees need to know what is expected of them as well as the outcomes of not complying with set expectations. This allows employees to practice self-discipline, or to act accordingly out of self-interest and a desire to meet these standards.

Positive discipline is the act of holding employees accountable in a way that encourages improved performance, learning, and growth. It is not meant to punish unless repeated poor performance occurs. Supervisors play a crucial role in the positive discipline process. Employees often take their cues from their supervisor's actions. If the supervisor fails to emulate what is expected of their employees, the impact of positive discipline will be greatly reduced.

Analyzing and Solving Job Performance Problems

Dealing with problem behavior is one of the greatest challenges you will have in your career. Many of us will avoid these issues as long as we can and often longer than we should. People can be unique, complex, and unpredictable. A major reason why we avoid dealing with these issues is because we have probably experienced failed attempts to change someone's behavior in the past and then had to experience the defensiveness and aggressiveness that often accompany attempts to deal with performance problems.

One of the main reasons why our attempt to correct poor performance fails is because we do not take the time to identify the real issue. We simply fail to identify the root cause of the issue. Reasons for such failures include:

- We often react according to our biases or assumptions about human nature.

- We act out of emotion and often become the aggressor instead of the mediator, which, in turn causes defensiveness on the part of the employee.

- We lay total blame on the employee without taking into account the fact that maybe they just did not understand or did not have the information they needed. It could even have been the result of a poor job design.

The good news is that there are techniques available to help us in analyzing these problems. We now present the steps necessary to analyze and solve job performance issues.

Problem Analysis — Focus Areas

Employees not doing what they should be doing:

1. What is the performance discrepancy? What is different

about what they are doing versus what they should be doing? Why am I upset and what is causing me to feel this way?

2. Is it important? What would happen if I did nothing? Will doing something to resolve the discrepancy lead to worthwhile results or could my actions result in unintended consequences?

3. Is it a skill deficiency? Could the person do the task under stricter requirements or with improved efforts? Are the person's present skills adequate for the desired performance?

4. Have they done it before? Could it be that their skills became rusty and they need to be retrained?

It is a skill deficiency:

1. How often do employees have to perform this particular task? Have they ever been given feedback on their performance in the past?

2. Is there a simpler solution? Can I change the job somehow? Could I do something as simple as an informal training to solve the problem?

3. Is the person capable of performing this task? Do they have the mental and physical skills necessary to complete it?

It is not a skill deficiency:

1. What is the consequence of performing as expected? Do the employees' efforts go unnoticed? Do they perceive that they are being punished for performing as expected? Do the employees even know and understand what their expectations are? What would happen if they performed better?

2. Is non-performance rewarded? What is the consequence of doing it the present way or not doing it at all? Does this

result in punishment or perceived rewards? Am I doing something that actually encourages the present way of doing things?

3. Does performing really matter to them? Are there any favorable outcomes (satisfaction) for performing or undesirable outcomes (counseling) for not performing?

4. Are there obstacles to performing? What prevents this person from performing? Does he/she know what is expected and when? Are there conflicting demands? Does he/she lack the time or authority to do the job? Am I standing in their way?

What should I do now?

When all meaningful solutions have been identified, the next step is to determine which solution is the best one. Ask yourself which solution addresses the real problem? What is the cost of the solution and is it even feasible to do it that way? What is the ease of implementation? Once you have identified the solution(s) which best aligns with both employee capabilities and organizational goals, take action to set it in place.

Performance Management Steps

Step 1. What is the performance discrepancy?

Behavior is rarely just a random act. It is helpful to think of all behavior as cause motivated and goal directed. When beginning to think about dealing with performance problems, think about problems objectively as differences between what people do and what someone wants them to do. Unfortunately we often take the simplistic view that "we have to teach them a lesson or they must change their behaviors."

First, think about what are the indicators of the problem. These include:

- They are not doing it the way they are supposed to.

- Absenteeism is too high.

- The supervisors are not motivated.

It is important to distinguish between a discrepancy and a deficiency. Discrepancies seemingly exist all the time. However, it is important that you resist jumping to conclusions without first determining if it is a true discrepancy or a deficiency.

Once you determine it is a discrepancy, it is important to identify and understand the nature of the discrepancy. What is the real problem? What we often think the problem is actually is not the problem at all but the symptom of a problem. Being late or absenteeism is often a symptom rather than a problem. Clearly, if one is going to spend a lot of time and effort solving a "problem," it is critical that the true problem is identified. Be clear on where there is a deviation from a standard. Identify how the problem affects others in the organization. Be clear on who is responsible for the problem.

Be careful not to jump to a solution too quickly. We often hear a manager say "we have a training problem." That is no different from a doctor saying "we have an aspirin problem." While that may be the solution, it usually is not the problem. Again, do not jump to conclusions until you have taken the time to identify the true problem.

Step 2: Is it important?

People perceive things differently (e.g., long hair, earrings). Ask yourself what the consequence would be if you left the problem alone. Try to calculate the cost or size of the discrepancy.

This involves assessing the consequences of performance discrepancies. Some areas to consider:

- Direct cost, intangible cost, time, material waste, equipment damage, accuracy, accidents, lost business, duplicated effort, extra supervision.

- Does the size of the gap between the actual and desired performance levels warrant any action to take place?

- What is the cost of eliminating the discrepancy?

If, after taking into consideration all of the above, the best solution is still to do nothing, then drop it. If the consequences of doing nothing are too large, though, then follow the same steps you did when conducting your Problem Analysis.

Take steps to determine if the deficiency is a result of:

- A skills deficiency

- Not using the skill often enough

- Too complex of an issue

- Not having what it takes to complete the job

- Perception of being punished for desired performance

- Rewarding non-performance

- Perception that performing just does not matter

- Obstacles to performing

If you were able to answer NO to all of the above questions, then the deficiency is probably the result of a failure to perform. You have a job performance issue which must be dealt with accordingly, up to and including discipline. Your next course of action is to conduct a root cause analysis to determine the reasons for the poor performance. The next section covers steps to take which will help with this determination.

The Disciplinary Action Process

The first step to take when it becomes apparent that a disciplinary action may be warranted is to conduct a pre-discipline interview. Bear in mind the following:

- Make it perfectly clear on what the purpose of the meeting is — to improve employee performance.

- Use the meeting to help the employee identify the problem, develop solutions, and understand that sustained inappropriate behavior will lead to increasingly harsher consequences. Keep the focus of the discussion on the problem, not the employee.

- Conduct the discipline interviews privately and promptly.

Record the results of the session and include the expected changes that must occur — then let the employee review it to ensure they have a clear understanding that doing nothing is not an option.

Remember that as a leader, your actions as well as your inactions will establish the standards for your team. Taking no action in the face of an obvious performance problem can be worse than taking the wrong action. Allowing poor performance to continue without direct involvement from you to correct the problem sets a new performance standard for that person as well as for other team members. You must tackle performance problems at once. It is hard work, but it is required work when in a leadership position.

Performance Counseling

Why Counsel an Employee?

Most performance problems can be resolved through effective communication between supervisors and their employees. A counseling session is an opportunity to clarify expectations and discuss performance problems.

What is the Difference Between Poor Performance and Misconduct?

Misconduct is generally a failure to follow a workplace rule. Examples of misconduct include a safety violation, tardiness and absenteeism, insubordination, and falsification.

Poor performance, on the other hand, is simply the failure of an employee to do the job at an acceptable level. The acceptable level is usually, but not always, documented in written performance standards and is typically defined in terms of quality, quantity, or timeliness. Although it is normal for performance and misconduct to be interrelated, it is important to recognize the difference between the two.

What is Effective Counseling?

If, despite taking preventive steps, you find that an employee's performance is still not meeting expectations, the best approach is to meet with the employee to discuss the problem.

Providing an Opportunity to Improve

In most cases, counseling sessions will prove very effective toward resolving poor performance. However, if an employee is still working at an unacceptable level even after counseling has taken place, it is time to take a more formal approach toward performance improvement.

Depending on the nature of the job and the employee's experience, this may be as simple as offering them assistance in performing their job. Examples of this include giving them a checklist to work with, pairing them with another more experienced employee, providing them training, or even overseeing their work and helping them with constructive feedback. Not every employee will require this type of assistance. However, once assistance is offered, be sure to follow through with it in a timely manner.

Opportunity To Improve

The procedures for providing a formal opportunity to improve include:

1. *Notice of a performance problem:* Inform the employee in writing that there is a performance problem and let them

know of the critical element(s) in which he or she is failing, what is needed to bring performance up to an acceptable level, what assistance will be provided, and the consequences of failing to improve within a specific time frame.

2. *Formal Opportunity to Improve*: Employee must bring performance up to an acceptable level in all of the failed areas. Duration of the opportunity period may vary. Be sure to document the employee's progress and to provide any appropriate assistance.

3. *Formal review of employee performance:* Employee's performance is evaluated throughout the opportunity period and then a formal review should be conducted at the end of the time frame they were given to improve.

Deciding What Comes Next

Deciding what comes next depends on the employee's performance at the conclusion of the opportunity period. If the employee has reached an acceptable level of performance, there is no need for any action except to keep providing feedback and encouragement to the employee. If the employee is still performing unacceptably, you must determine the next steps. Ask yourself the following questions to help determine where you go from here.

What is my responsibility to the employee when there is a performance issue?

As the employee's supervisor, it is your responsibility to keep an employee regularly informed about his or her performance, particularly when that assessment is negative. When performance gets to the point where formal action must be taken, follow the guidelines provided in your employee handbook or any other policy or practice established for your organization. If there are none, or you still are not sure, contact your human resources department for help.

Should I wait for the annual performance appraisal to tell an employee that his or her performance is unacceptable?

No, you should not wait. In fact, good leaders provide their employees with performance feedback throughout the appraisal cycle as we discussed in the previous step.

I never counseled an employee before. What kind of information do I need in order to prepare for a counseling meeting?

One of the most important documents you will need is a copy of the employee's job description. This is important from the standpoint of being able to identify those areas where their performance does not align with job expectations. In addition, have a copy of any company policy or work practice that the employee is not in compliance with. You will also need copies of any notes you may have taken regarding their performance up to that point, prior discussions you may have had with them concerning their performance, goals you may have set for them, follow up meetings you had with them, and the outcomes of those meetings just to name a few.

One of the most important things to remember in taking notes is to date them so they reflect when you met with an employee or when you noted both good and bad performance. When logging poor performance, be sure to note specific examples of what they were doing that failed to meet expectations. Doing so will make it easier for you to explain the performance issue(s) to the employee when you meet with him or her.

Effective Counseling Tips

Following are the tips to help you prepare for and conduct effective counseling sessions:

- Before counseling, make sure you can clearly define what would constitute acceptable performance.

- Make sure that you conduct the counseling session in a private place.

- Arrange adequate time for the meeting to ensure that both you and the employee have the necessary time for comments.

- Clearly state performance expectations and seek confirmation that the employee understands those expectations.

- Focus on the poor performance, not on the person or their personalities.

- Always maintain a constructive tone of voice along with a calm and professional demeanor.

- Seek cooperation, NOT confrontation.

- Remember that your goal is to improve the employee's performance, not to win an argument with the employee.

- Try to end the session on a positive note by emphasizing that your goal is to improve the employee's performance.

In closing, employees want to know where they stand in terms of performance, both good and bad. As a leader, it is your responsibility to provide regular and meaningful performance feedback to all of your employees. If employees are performing well, tell them so they know to continue doing so. On the other hand, they "cannot fix it if they do not know it is broken."

If they are not performing according to expectations, tell them so and give them the opportunity to correct themselves prior to the year-end formal appraisal. Giving performance feedback takes time, but if you truly care about the well-being of your employees, the return on investment will be more than worth the time you put into letting them know how they are doing.

Maximizing Employee Performance

Getting the most from your employees is at the heart of our definition of leadership. As a leader, you should not be content with the status quo. Instead, you should constantly seek to improve performance through motivation, inspiration, and leading by example.

The Ten Keys to Maximizing Employee Performance

1. *Let people know what you expect.* If people know what is expected of them, that is what they will do. If they do not know what is expected, they will do something else. Communicate clear and unambiguous performance expectations and hold people accountable for their performance.

2. *Be a systems thinker.* Remind people that what they do in one area could affect others in multiple areas. If people know how their actions impact others, they will try harder to perform well.

3. *Keep people informed on current events.* Do not assume they can read your mind. If there is something going on that could impact them, let them know. If people do not know, they invent and the human tendency is to assume the negative. A well-timed word on your part will prevent a lot of worry on theirs.

4. *Let people 'own' their jobs.* Do you remember your first car; how you felt about owning it; and how hard you worked to keep it clean and in good running order? The same holds true for people's jobs. If people feel like they "own" their job, they will work harder to polish and preserve it.

5. *Establish a culture of feedback.* Things typically go wrong only 10 percent of the time yet we spend 90 percent of our time belaboring those things that went wrong. On the other

hand, we probably spend 10 percent of our time talking about the 90 percent of the time we did things well. This is a normal occurrence when providing feedback as well. Spending more time providing feedback about the positive outcomes makes it easier to talk to people about the negatives. Letting people know when they did well does not diminish your authority as a leader in any way. Feedback truly is the breakfast of champions and people who feel like champions act like champions.

6. *Share your power.* When we are given power, there is an expectation that we will use it responsibly. People who use power responsibly do not manipulate or intimidate. Instead, they focus on what they can give to others rather than on what they can get. They share their power, or empower others to help make decisions and provide influence. Like the common parable about "casting your bread upon the waters," the return is a thousand fold. Those with whom the power is shared give it back in greater measure and the mutual ability to influence is enhanced. Simply put, power shared is power gained.

7. The coach, not the players, is usually the first to get fired when a sports team performs poorly. Surprisingly, the coach is usually "relieved" by the players and not the general manager. While this sounds crazy, when a coach fails to motivate employees to provide maximum effort, players will typically perform only good enough to keep their jobs. The coach then is held accountable for not providing a championship season. So it is in the business world.

8. *Money is not always the answer.* As with a prized athlete, if you take their pay away they will not show up for the game. But offering them more does nothing to make them work or play harder either.

9. *Treat your people like volunteers.* Have you ever noticed how hard volunteers work, how dedicated most of them

are, how much time they give to their volunteer organizations? This is usually because others recognize and appreciate their skills. Often volunteers are given important jobs that carry large responsibility. Recognition and opportunity are what drive volunteers. Treat the people who work with you like volunteers and the results will amaze you.

10. *What happens while you are there does not matter.* It is what happens when you are not there that counts. Build a sense of trust in your employees and they will do what is right all the time.

When an employee's work output fails to meet performance standards, the leader must discover the reasons why. But what happens when the leader lacks the ability to successfully determine the reasons for such shortcomings?

Inexperienced supervisors probably have the most difficulty in correcting problems that involve under-performing staff members. One reason inexperienced supervisors often have difficulty with problem resolution in situations involving people is because it is never easy. In fact, it is typically a challenge to "manage" problems that involve employees rather than lead the employees to a solution. Each person has his or her own attitude, viewpoint, and perspective. As a new or inexperienced supervisor, you are often dealing with "friends"or people you have recently worked alongside. That can add to the difficulties of managing employee problems since many employees may not yet "recognize" you as the boss or may think that you will approach the issue the same as if you were still working in your previous position.

Many observers note that one of the most important responsibilities of a supervisor is the one that involves employees. Managing equipment, products, materials, time, and money are absolutely critical. However, the majority of the work in most departments is performed by employees. Learning strategies that will help quickly identify potential problems can give the supervisor a jump start when developing problem resolution strategies.

Chapter 12

The Art of Leadership

Teaching and Training

The art of leadership really boils down to learning and practicing people skills. Your ability to interact with your employees on a relational level will largely determine how effective you are in training, teaching, coaching, motivating, mentoring, and inspiring them toward success.

Demonstrate Enthusiasm: In many ways, you set the tone for your employees. If you are unmotivated, expect your employees to be unmotivated as well. Likewise, if you demonstrate enthusiasm for your work, it will carry over to your employees.

Interface with your Employees: It is important that you interact directly with your employees on a regular basis. A prolonged pattern of not doing so creates the perception that you are a cold, uncaring autocrat rather than the caring, compassionate leader you want to be. Step out from behind that desk periodically and let your employees interact with you face to face.

Celebrate Accomplishments: Take time out to celebrate accomplishments as a company. When you have asked your employees to go the extra mile to complete a major project, it is not unreasonable for them to expect something in return. This can be as simple as ordering a pizza or as extravagant as organizing an annual holiday party outside of the office. What you do is not as important as recognizing a job well done.

Offer Incentives: With incentives, cash is not always king. Sometimes the best incentives require a little creativity on your part. In addition to offering flexitime for employees who demonstrate outstanding service and performance, you can do things like offer theater tickets or restaurant gift certificates to the "employee of the month." Part of the fun is creating an atmosphere where your employees do not know what their reward will be until they have achieved their goal.

Treat your Employees with Kindness: Kindness and understanding on your part will go a long way toward motivating your employees to help you achieve your goals. While unplanned events such as sick kids or other personal crises can interfere with the daily flow of the workplace, no matter how many problems these occurrences cause for you, you can be guaranteed that they have created many more problems for your employees. As much as possible, try to give your employees the time they need to care for their families. You will end up with happier employees who are more likely to go the extra mile for you when you need it most.

Listen: Above all else, listen to what your employees have to say and let them know how much you value their input. The loyalty it inspires in your employees will make it well worth your while.

Train and Teach

One of the most frustrating situations for an employee is to be assigned a task that they do not know how to do. Set your team up for success by ensuring that all are trained and ready to do their jobs.

In switching gears, do you remember your first day on a job? Were you confident about this new experience or were you anxious and perhaps apprehensive? Most people starting a new job would admit to being nervous as well as being concerned about performing their duties up to their employer's standards along with being accepted by other employees. Supervisors often neglect to adequately give orientation and train new employees. They assume the new employees understand what needs to be done or will "catch on" quickly. Employee orientation and training programs are the most important things you will ever do for an employee. First impressions last a lifetime. But when you take the time to truly welcome an employee to your company by spending the time necessary to help them overcome their initial concerns and anxieties, it will go far towards making them feel a part of the team which will, in turn, increase worker productivity, decrease confusion, and increase satisfaction for both employer and employee.

The orientation of a new employee can involve several people even though one person has overall responsibility. Orientation will change from business to business, but the basics that should be discussed with the new employee include the values of the organization and the specific characteristics of the business (layout of facilities, other employees, history, mission, goals, and role of employee). This kind of information provides the "big picture" of the business to the new employee. Personnel policies, disciplinary actions, work schedules, safety rules, and use of equipment also need to be covered. New employees are always interested in their benefits. Cover items such as pay, paydays, vacation, sick leave, and other benefits. Give them a copy of your employee handbook containing these and other policies to ensure that they are clear on what their expectations are.

Discuss specific job responsibilities the new employee will be assigned along with how their job relates to other work performed in the business. Finally, be sure to introduce the new employee to other employees within the business.

Answer all of the immediate questions that the new employee might have. It is important to develop open, two-way lines of communication between the employer and employee right from the beginning. Consider the time spent for orientation as an investment for both you and the employee. Clear, well-defined expectations will pay dividends in the future and reduce possible misunderstandings between employer and employee.

Training

Do you expect your new employees to already be trained when they show up for their first day on the job? Too often supervisors hope for a "ready to hit the ground running" employee. It is unrealistic to believe that all new employees have the abilities and skills necessary to do the required tasks to your standards.

The first thing you will need to do is to conduct a skills analysis on the new employee to determine what their knowledge, skills, and abilities are. This can be done by reviewing their job application or resume, having a discussion with them concerning their employment history, following up with their references, or observing them as they perform their daily duties.

Once you determine training needs for the new employee and have a training plan in place, discuss with them what outcomes are expected of the training. Include such factors as speed and accuracy, performance standards and levels deemed satisfactory for completing various tasks. If available, give them a copy of the standard operating procedures for each task which could contain such things as the chronological order for completing the tasks.

The role of supervisor or trainer becomes one of a teacher in the training process. The ability to teach the employee a particular skill or task is critical if training goals are to be met. Most find a step-by-step process the most successful in training employees.

Typical Reasons for Employee Training and Development

Training and development can be initiated for a variety of reasons for an employee or group of employees:

- When a performance appraisal indicates performance improvement is needed.

- To "benchmark" the status of improvement in a performance improvement effort.

- As part of an overall professional development or succession planning program to help prepare employees for planned changes or roles within the organization.

- To "pilot" or test the operation of a new performance management system.

- When employees have no prior experience operating newly acquired equipment.

- To train on a specific topic.

Typical Topics of Employee Training

Communications: The increasing diversity of today's workforce brings a wide variety of languages and customs.

Computer skills: Computer skills are becoming a necessity for conducting administrative and office tasks.

Customer service: Increased competition in today's global marketplace makes it critical that employees understand and meet the needs of customers.

Diversity: Diversity training usually includes explanations on people's differing perspectives and views, and includes techniques on how to respect and value diversity.

Ethics: Today's society has increasing expectations about corporate social responsibility. Also, today's diverse workforce brings a wide variety of values and morals to the workplace.

Human relations: The increased stresses of today's workplace can cause misunderstandings and conflict. Training can teach people on how to overcome issues such as these and to get along in the workplace.

Quality initiatives: Initiatives such as Total Quality Management, Quality Circles, Benchmarking, etc., require basic training about quality concepts, guidelines and standards for quality.

Safety: Safety training is critical where working with heavy equipment, new equipment, hazardous chemicals, repetitive activities, etc. It can also be a useful tool for giving practical advice on avoiding assaults.

Sexual harassment: Sexual harassment training usually includes explicit explanations of the organization's policies about sexual harassment, including such things as what inappropriate behaviors are.

General Benefits from Employee Training & Development

The reasons for supervisors to conduct training among employees include:

- Increased job satisfaction and morale among employees.
- Increased employee motivation.
- Increased efficiencies in processes, resulting in financial gain.
- Increased capacity to adopt new technologies and methods.
- Increased innovation in strategies and products.
- Reduced employee turnover.

- Enhanced company image (through ethics training, for example).

- Risk management (through sexual harassment and diversity training).

Some Contemporary Principles of Adult Learning

The process of action learning is based on contemporary views of adult learning. Action learning asserts that adults learn best when:

- Working to address a current, real-world problem.

- They are highly vested in solving the current problem.

- They actually apply new materials and information.

- They provide ongoing feedback centered on their experiences.

In addition, adults often learn best from experience rather than from extensive note taking and memorization.

To Learn, You Must Be Willing to Grow and to Experience

Learning often involves new skills and new behaviors. After many years of classroom education, it is easy for us to take a course where all we must do is attend each session, take notes, and pass tests. We can complete a Master's in Business Administration (MBA) program, but unless we are willing to actually apply new knowledge, we will most likely end up with an office full of unreferenced textbooks and a head full of data, but little practical knowledge and wisdom. This is not learning. This is simply the art of remembering.

For the learning process to succeed, we must be willing to take risks. If the training or learning does not meet your expectations, let someone know about it as soon as you can. Do not wait until the course is over and nothing can be done about it.

Growth Involves the Entire Learner

If our learning is to be more than just a collection of new information, we must become active participants in the learning experience. Unfortunately, too many development program providers still operate from the assumption that the learner's personal development does not matter as much as their professional development. They separate that out of the training they provide. So we end up getting a great deal of information about specific items such as finance and sales, for example, but very little help with personal development necessities such as stress and time management. Then, after the completion of learning, we enter the hectic world of management and struggle to maintain order and are plagued with self-doubt.

True learning involves looking at every aspect of our lives, not just what is in our heads. Teaching people about things like Stress Management and Emotional Intelligence are very important to your overall training and development plans, so make sure you look for programs that incorporate both hard and soft skills training.

Growth Requires Seeking Ongoing Feedback

Many of us do not know what we need to learn — we do not know what we do not know. Therefore, feedback from others is critical to understanding ourselves and our jobs. Feedback is useful in more ways than just telling someone what they do not know or what they are doing wrong. Feedback also deepens and enriches what we do know and those things we are doing right.

Research indicates that adults learn new information and methods best when they a) actually apply the knowledge and methods, and b) exchange feedback around those experiences. However, we are often reluctant to seek advice and feedback from others, particularly fellow workers. We are sometimes reluctant to share feedback with others, as well.

The courage to overcome our reluctance and fear is often the first step toward achieving true growth in our lives and our jobs.

Include Learners in Training and Development Planning

Learners are often the best experts at realizing their own needs for self-development. Therefore, learners should be involved in developing their training and development plan as much as possible. People take more ownership when they feel like they are a part of the process or planning. In addition, professional growth rarely encompasses merely learning new skills and abilities. Self-development, or people skills, are just as important, and sometimes more important than learning how to do a new task.

If Available, Have Human Resources Representative Play Major Role

A trained human resources professional can be a major benefit in employee development. The representative usually has a good understanding of the dynamics of training and development. They also have a strong working knowledge of the relevant policies and procedures related to training and development. In addition, the representative can be an impartial confidant for the learner.

Provide Ongoing Feedback and Support

Some learners may not feel comfortable asking for help. Even if things seem to be going fine, supervisors still need to check in with the learner regularly to see if there are questions or concerns as well as provide feedback that is useful for the learner. Provide ongoing affirmation and support.

Assessing Employee Learning and Maximizing Feedback

Consider getting feedback from the learner's peers and subordinates about the learner's progress. A 360-degree performance review is a powerful practice when carried out with clarity and discretion, and when used correctly. It might be wise to consider bringing in a professional the first time you use this tool to ensure that both you and the employees understand the intent and usefulness of it.

Coaching and Mentoring

As leaders, we tend to get wrapped up in the day-to-day operations of our organization and we do not take time to plan for our own career moves, which could include retirement. We do not take the time to develop someone to replace us. You need to take a hard look at whether there is someone on your team who could readily assume your leadership role if you are gone on vacation, move to another department, get promoted, or retire. If not, then you should seriously consider mentoring and coaching your employee(s) to get them ready for this potential situation.

Poor or misinformed leaders think that if they train someone to do their jobs, they will then become vulnerable to being fired. That is typically not the case. Instead, by building your subordinate(s) up so that they can perform in your absence, creates a win-win situation for you, your key employees, and the organization as a whole. This is the hallmark of effective leadership — doing what needs to be done even though you are not there to supervise them. Coaching and mentoring is more than just "selecting your replacement." It involves bringing out the best in your team members in order to improve performance and create a learning atmosphere within your team.

The Supervisor as a Coach

A good supervisor places a high priority on coaching employees. Good coaching involves working with employees to establish suitable goals, action plans and time lines. The supervisor delegates and also provides ongoing guidance and support to the employees as they complete their action plans. Rarely can job goals be established without considering other aspects of an employee's life. Take time to discuss such things as training, career goals, personal strengths and weaknesses, and so forth with them. If their career goals include areas for which they have no skills or they aspire to a position for which you know they will never be a viable candidate, be honest with them and let them know that. This is sometimes a hard discussion to have with them, but they will thank you for it later.

The Supervisor as a Mentor

Usually the supervisor understands the organization and the employee's profession better than the employee does. Consequently, the supervisor is in a unique position to give ongoing advice to the employee about their job and career. The employee can look to the supervisor as a great resource for direction and guidance. An effective mentor-mentee relationship requires the supervisor to accept the responsibility of mentorship and then follow through on it. A good supervisor can be a priceless addition to the career of an employee.

What Mentoring Means

Mentoring encompasses the technical, professional, and personal development of our only source of sustainable corporate advantage — people. A mentor willingly devotes his or her time, talent, and energy to helping people develop and fulfill their career potential.

The word *mentor* has roots in *The Odyssey* of ancient Greek mythology. When Odysseus left Ithaca to fight in the Trojan War, he entrusted Mentor with the care and development of his son *Telemachus*. After the war, *Odysseus* wandered for ten years, trying to return home. In his search for his father, *Telemachus* was accompanied by *Athena*, who assumed the form of *Mentor*.

Mentor's wise counsel, tutelage, and guardianship resonate through today's workplace *mentoring* practices. Over time, mentoring has become synonymous with the guidance and support offered by a trusted, more experienced adviser — someone who takes an active, influential, yet usually informal interest in guiding a *protégé's* progress within the organization's political culture.

Think back to your first day at work. Did you wake up that morning wanting to be a poor performer? Was it your ambition to be just *average*? It is more likely you were motivated to excel, but were not completely sure about how to do that. By trial and error, you made sense of the ambiguity and unwritten rules of the real world. Maybe you even had a supervisor with the attitude that "I had to learn the hard way. So can everyone else." Hopefully that was not the case and instead you had leaders or even more experienced peers who took the time to share their expertise and show you the ropes.

It is clear that we can no longer afford the sink or swim approach. This ruins relationships, imperils dedication, reduces confidence, and wastes resources. This type of organization WILL NOT attract people, investors, and customers in today's business climate. Instead, becoming an organization that provides for a structured, long-term approach to developing and supporting high potential achievers will open many doors and attract high performers and committed investors and customers. Mentors support the development of a protégé's mastery of the following dimensions.

Manage knowledge

Mentors can play a pivotal role in ensuring the success of an organization's strategic learning and development initiatives. By developing mentoring skills, leaders gain credibility by helping people use what they have learned during formal learning activities to develop their long-term career potential. With this support and guidance, people will develop the confidence and commitment they need to achieve individual goals and support organizational goals and strategies. Remember, setbacks and failures can be equally valuable experiences if we learn from them, help others learn from them, and use this knowledge to improve our performance.

Ease Transition to New Responsibilities

Mentors help people with new roles or additional assignments in order to get up to speed more quickly by helping them to understand the organization's expectations and to learn the unwritten *'tricks of the trade'* for those specific roles or assignments. Mentors can also help people to minimize failure and setbacks by sharing their own experiences and the experiences of others who have faced similar challenges. By taking an active interest in developing their mentees, mentors can help people avoid common pitfalls and develop the values, commitment, and skills they need to succeed.

Networking and Best Practice Communities

Mentors exchange ideas, stimulate dialogue, and enhance skills by creating a support network of other experienced practitioners and managers. They share with others what has or has not worked for them.

Mentors believe in a level playing field for everyone. They recognize that superior performance merits special recognition and reward. They help people to realize their career aspirations and personal potential by clarifying expectations and presenting realistic, credible career development options. They help people assume responsibility for their own development and commit themselves to giving their best performance.

Organized mentoring programs have enhanced individual performance through greater career satisfaction and retention, better decision making, and higher levels of personal commitment.

Although issues related to employment conditions should be handled through established procedures, culture and practices can and do impact performance. Helping high potential performers understand what they must do to improve, and the consequences of not doing so, through effective and timely mentoring can be a catalyst for turning problem performers into superior performers. This should be done *before* performance issues adversely impact their career prospects and *before* a formal intervention becomes necessary.

Retain and develop talent

Mentoring facilitates continuity in management succession and retention of skilled talent by identifying achievers with leadership potential and technical skills. Organized and leadership focused approaches to mentoring develop the visibility, skills, and all around capabilities of these high potential people. They also provide them the tools they need to assume additional responsibility and to have rewarding careers within the organization.

Guide

Although the mentors may not have all the answers, mentors can share valuable insights gained through their own experiences to give vision, purpose, direction, focus, and meaning to a protégé's career development. Mentors may also ask thought-provoking questions and honest feedback which will help challenge pre-conceived assumptions and complacency on the part of the mentee. This helps to stimulate fresh insights and perspectives on organizational, political, or social realities, thereby sharpening a protégé's critical thinking, problem solving, and decision-making skills.

Guardian

By helping them to learn how to discern the risks inherent in any course of action, mentors protect protégés from avoidable corporate and career mistakes. This guidance helps them avoid the rocks and shoals upon which their career advancement may be founded. By suggesting alternatives and helping protégés plan their development more effectively, mentors protect the interests of the protégé and the organization.

Advocate

Mentors actively represent mentees' interests, introduce them to key people, identify opportunities for them to visibly showcase their talents and capabilities, and share responsibility — and credit — for joint achievements.

Confidant

Mentors serve as a sounding board for the protégé to confidentially test new ideas, share insights, discuss workplace issues or vent frustrations. They listen with genuine interest, concern, and empathy, exploring and reflecting on issues before offering their own judgements. Most importantly, they build and create a level of trust with the protégé by ensuring confidentiality throughout the mentoring relationship.

Protégé Roles And Responsibilities

Protégés bring their own qualities, views, and talents to the mentoring arena. As the relationship evolves, their perspectives, commitment and passion can make a real difference.

The 16 Laws of Mentoring

1. *The Law of Positive Environment:* Create a positive environment where potential and motivation are released and options discussed.

2. *The Law of Developing Character:* Nurture a positive character by helping to develop not just talent, but a wealth of mental and ethical traits.

3. *The Law of Shared Mistakes*: Share your failures as well as your successes.

4. *The Law of Planned Objectives:* Prepare specific goals for your relationship.

5. *The Law of Independence:* Promote autonomy; make the learner independent of you, not dependent on you.

6. *The Law of Limited Responsibility*: Be responsible to them, not for them.

7. *The Law of Inspection*: Monitor, review, critique, and discuss potential actions. Do not just expect performance without inspection.

8. *The Law of Tough Love*: The participants acknowledge the need to encourage independence in the learner.

9. *The Law of Small Successes:* Use a stepping-stone process to build on accomplishments and achieve great success.

10. *The Law of Direction*: It is important to teach by providing options as well as direction.

11. *The Laws of Risk*: A mentor should be aware that a learner's failure may reflect back upon him/her. A learner should realize that a mentor's advice will not always work.

12. *The Law of Mutual Protection*: Commit to covering each other's backs. Maintain privacy. Protect integrity, character, and the pearls of wisdom you have shared with one another.

13. *The Law of Communication*: The mentor and the learner must balance listening and delivering information.

14. *The Law of Extended Commitment*: The mentoring relationship extends beyond the typical 8-to-5 business day and/or traditional workplace role or position.

15. *The Law of Life Transition*: As a mentor, when you help a learner enter the next stage of his/her life or career, you will enter the next stage of yours as well.

16. *The Law of Fun*: Make mentoring a wonderful experience — laugh, smile, and enjoy the process.

Motivating and Inspiring

Think back to the definition of leadership and you see the words "motivate" and "inspire." How do you do this? What should you do (and not do) with your employees to motivate them? In this section, we will discuss techniques to motive and inspire employee performance. Much has been written about this subject and by no means is this section all inclusive. Rather, think of this section as a starting point from which to refine your motivational and inspirational competencies.

We all know people who have inspired us. For some of us it might have been a family member. For others maybe it was a historical or religious figure. People who started a small business and built it into multi-million dollar empires inspire many of us who own or would like to own our own company. For kids, it might be an imaginary hero from a book or movie. Of course, most of us in America were inspired by the actions of the heroes of September 11th. In thinking along these lines, how can we, as managers, learn to inspire others?

Start with the examples of those people who inspired you and what you learned from them. Ask yourself how and why they inspired you? Once you have reflected on your own heroes, you can then use that to motivate and inspire your team to become the best they can be. In conclusion, inspire your employees to become the best they can be by practicing the following examples of leadership best practices.

Be A Good Example

"Do as I say, not as I do" is not good advice for managers. Employees will always watch what you do more than they listen to what you say. They will not only focus on what you do at work, but when not there as well. Do not be hypocritical. Be someone worth following.

Appreciate Your Employees

Everyone likes to be appreciated for the work they do. Employees like to feel as if they are a valued part of the company, which will also help them do their best. Offer public praise and recognize victories often, and make it authentic.

Share Your Failures

By being willing to share your failures as well as your successes, others will relate to you much easier and more deeply. They will understand that they are not the only people with challenges, that success does not come overnight, and it is not without problems.

Watch What You Say

Watch what you say and how you say it. While we may not intend to come across in a certain way, it is easy to become condescending when relating how you have overcome problems or how you have succeeded (and they did not). This also includes written communication and especially e-mail.

Challenge Your Employees

If you ever had a teacher or a mentor who challenged you, you will understand what this means. They asked you to go the extra mile and to do your best. It might have been difficult and you probably did not think you could do it, but believe it or not, more often than not you made it and were grateful for the push.

Motivate Them By Caring, Not Scaring

Fear should never be used as a motivation strategy. It may get you what you want now, but it will come back to haunt you in the future in the form of employee anger, resentment, and lack of enthusiasm and commitment. When employees feel that managers care about them and that they are perceived as respected and valuable members of the organization, they are more cooperative, enthusiastic, and committed to succeed, both in the present and in the future.

Growth And Blossoming of Employee Motivation In The Right Environment

The job of the manager is to create a work environment that provides employees with the opportunity to attain their goals and experience what they value most in their professional lives. In this environment, communication is open and honest, coaching for success is ongoing, training for performance improvement is continuous, and creative problem-solving is a way of life. Managers also need to provide sincere expressions of recognition, appreciation, and acknowledge-ment to nourish their employees' feelings of self-worth.

Walk Your Talk

Modeling the behavior you want from your employees is the most effective way to change their and everyone else's behavior. If you want your employees to arrive on time, you should be in early. If you want motivated employees, you need to be motivated yourself. Regardless of what it is that you want and expect from your employees, remember, most people will never become motivated or strive to succeed when presented with tasks that you, as a manager, are not committed to on a personal and professional level.

Make Work Fun!

The research is clear. Laughter is not only good for the soul, but for the mind and body as well. Having fun is a basic human need, and when it is met in the workplace, productivity goes up. Appoint a "fun" committee and come up with ways to bring enjoyment into your department.

Bringing fun into the workplace lowers stress levels and provides opportunities for employees to build rapport with each other, which is the foundation for successful team-building.

The Law of Attraction

The law of attraction states that whatever we focus on, we bring it to ourselves. If you focus on the lack of motivation in your employees, you will find more and more examples of it. When you seek to learn more about motivation and create an atmosphere that fosters it, you will find more motivated employees in the workplace.

Ongoing Commitment

Mentoring and truly caring about your employees is an ongoing process because people are continually growing and changing. As they achieve something they want or value, they then seek to achieve more of the same, to move to that next level. If motivation is not kept on your managerial front burner, you will see the fires in your employees slowly fade and die out.

Strategic Leadership

"The best executive is the one who has the sense enough to pick good men to do what he wants done and self-restraint enough to keep from meddling with them while they do it." Theodore Roosevelt, 26th President of the United States.

Executive leaders guide the achievement of their organizational vision by acquiring and allocating resources, directing policy, building consensus, influencing organizational culture, and shaping complex and usually ambiguous internal and external environments.

Executive leaders lead by example to build effective organizations, grow the next generation of leaders, energize subordinates, seek opportunities to advance organizational goals, and balance personal and professional demands.

Strategic Leadership Challenges

Maintain Your Perspective: Consider the entire organization, not just a particular functional area. Be careful not to become so engaged in the details that you lose your objectivity.

Anticipate and Shape the Future: Know and understand the time frame in which you operate. Engage external stakeholders to shape the future environment.

Stay In Your Lane: Let supervisors and managers run the organization. Your job is to synchronize processes and systems across the organization.

Clear Communications with Key Messages: The Vision is your message. Clearly and consistently articulate a few powerful messages that communicate the Vision.

Consider 2nd and 3rd Order Effects of Decisions: Effects have causes. Effects can, and usually do, become causes of other effect(s) and because of this, there can be a large number of cause and effect "chains" created based on a single causal event.

Final Thoughts

Here There Be Dragons....

In ancient times, mapmakers did not have a clear and certain view of the world. Instead, they only knew about what the explorers told them was out there. The notes and charts the explorers maintained were used to draw the maps that would be employed by future explorers. On the other side of the known world, these cartographers would often draw sea monsters and dragons to symbolize the unknowns: *here there be dragons.*

Leadership is about slaying these dragons and turning the unknown into the known. Leaders are people who thrive on tackling change, dealing with uncertainty and complex problems, and truly making the significant differences needed in order to propel others forward into the land of the unknowns: *here there be dragons.*

It has often been said that management is concerned with doing things right, whereas leadership is concerned with doing the right things. If that is true, then management is focused on making the map correct whereas leadership is concerned with discovering what else is out there that other explorers missed: *here there be dragons.*

So, go forth and lead boldly! Never give up, never quit. Never give in to the temptations and revert to the path of least resistance. Instead, go out and slay some dragons. After all, that is what leadership is all about: *here there be dead dragons.*

References and
Selected Bibliography

Abrashoff, D.M. (2002). *It's Your Ship.* New York, NY: Warner Books, Inc.

Barber, B.E. (2004). *No Excuse Leadership: Lessons from the U.S. Army's Elite Rangers.* Hoboken, NJ: John Wiley & Sons, Inc.

Canfield, J., Hansens, M.V., Rogerson, M., Rutte, M., & Clauss, T. (1996). *Chicken Soup for the Soul at Work.* Deerfield Beach, FL: Health Communications, Inc.

Carrison, D., & Walsh, R. (1999). *Semper Fi: Business Leadership the Marine Corps Way.* New York, NY: American Management Association.

Center for Army Leadership (2004). *The U.S. Army Leadership Field Manual: Battle-Tested Wisdom for Leadership in Any Organization.* New York, NY: McGraw-Hill.

Collins, J. (2001). *Good to Great: Why some Companies Make the Leap and Others Don't.* New York, NY: HarperCollins Publishers, Inc.

Collins, J. & Hansen, M.T. (2011). *Great by Choice.* New York, NY: HarperCollins Publishers, Inc.

Connelly, O. (2002). *On War and Leadership: The Words of Combat Commanders from Frederick the Great to Norman Schwarzkopf.* Princeton, NJ: Princeton University Press.

Covey, S.R. (2004). *The 8th Habit: From Effectiveness to Greatness.* New York, NY: Simon & Schuster, Inc.

Drucker, P. (1966). *The Effective Executive.* New York, NY: Harper & Row.

Harvard Business Essentials. (2004). *Creating Teams with an Edge: The Complete Skill Set to Build Powerful and Influential Teams.* Boston, MA: Harvard Business School Publishing Corporation.

Huszczo, G. (2004). *Tools for Team Leadership: Delivering the X Factor in Team Excellence.* Palo Alto, CA: Davies-Black Publishing.

Kotter, J.P. (1996). *Leading Change.* Boston, MA: Harvard Business School Press.

Lakein, A. (1974). *How to Get Control of Your Time and Your Life.* New York, NY: Signet.

Maxwell, J.C. (2004). *Developing the Leaders Within You: Workbook.* Nashville, TN: Thomas Nelson, Inc.

Maxwell, J.C. (2005). *The 360° Leader: Developing Your Influence from Anywhere.* Nashville, TN: Thomas Nelson, Inc.

Maxwell, J.C. (2001). *The 17 Indisputable Laws of Teamwork: Embrace Them and Empower Your Team.* Nashville, TN: Thomas Nelson, Inc.

Maxwell, J.C. (2000). *The 21 Most Powerful Minutes in a Leaders Day: Revitalize Your Sprit and Empower Your Leadership.* Nashville, TN: Thomas Nelson, Inc.

McConnel, T. (1974). *Group Leadership for Self-Realization.* London, England: Mason and Lipscomb Publishers.

McDeilly, M. (2001). *Sun Tzu and The Art of Modern Warfare.* New York, NY: Oxford University Press, Inc.

McGee-Cooper, A. (1983). *Time Management for Unmanageable People.* Dallas, TX: Ann McGee-Cooper & Associates.

Nanus, B. (1992). *Visionary Leadership.* New York, NY: Maxwell Macmillan International Publishing.

Santamaria, J.A., Martino, V., & Clemens, E.K. (2004). *The Marine Corps Way: Using Maneuver Warfare to Lead A Winning Organization.* New York, NY: McGraw-Hill Publishing.

Snair, S. (2004). *West Point Leadership Lessons: Duty Honor and Other Management Principles.* Naperville, IL: Sourcebooks, Inc.

Tichy, N.M. (2002). *The Cycle of Leadership: How Great Leaders Teach their Companies to Win.* New York, NY: HarperCollins Publishers, Inc.

Welch, J., & Welch, S. (2005). *Winning.* New York, NY: HarperCollins Publishers, Inc.

Brief Biography of the Authors

Olin O. Oedekoven, Ph.D.

Dr. Olin Oedekoven has an extensive background in leadership, organizational development, higher education, strategic planning, and institutional evaluation. His undergraduate degree is in Wildlife and Fisheries Management (South Dakota State University), and his first Master's degree is in Wildlife Ecology (University of Wyoming). Olin then worked in state government as a Natural Resource Specialist for 20 years.

Olin continued his formal education with Northcentral University, earning an MBA and a Ph.D. in Business Administration with concentrations in Management and Public Administration. He later earned a post-doctoral certification in Human Resource Management. Dr. Oedekoven taught doctoral level students for 10 years, including chairing approximately 40 Ph.D. committees.

Concurrently, Dr. Oedekoven served for nearly 33 years in the U.S. Army Reserves and U.S. Army National Guard. He retired in 2011 as the Deputy Adjutant General of the Wyoming National Guard, leading an organization that included nearly 3,500 members (civilian and uniformed employees). Brigadier

General Oedekoven has a Master's degree in Strategic Planning from the U.S. Army War College, and served on several U.S. government councils and committees during his tenure as a general officer.

Dr. Oedekoven founded Peregrine Leadership Institute in 2003 and Peregrine Academic Services in 2009. The Leadership Institute provides leadership development training, organizational assessment, strategic planning assistance, and executive leadership seminars. Highlights associated with the leadership development services include management training throughout the U.S. with government and private sector organizations, ongoing leadership training in Canada, and leadership development work in China, Tunisia, Mongolia, Vietnam, India, and Ghana.

Peregrine Academic Services provides online assessment and educational services to institutions of higher education throughout the world. Services include program-level assessments in disciplines such as business, early childhood education, public administration, and accounting/finance. Peregrine has consulted with both governmental and academic institutions and organizations concerning higher education needs, compliance, academic accreditation, assurance of learning, quality, and reform. In 2012-2013, Dr. Oedekoven conducted several strategic planning and executive-level leadership seminars for the Accreditation Council for Business Schools and Programs.

John E. Lavrenz, MBA

John has 30+ years of experience at all organizational levels. He has a comprehensive background in the areas of training and development and has extensive experience in the areas of leadership, organizational development, affirmative action, succession planning, HR management, labor relations, and project management.

John has an undergraduate degree in Business Management with a concentration in Organizational Psychology and a Master's degree in Business Administration with a concentration in Project Management. He has served on numerous boards and has been instrumental in helping with program development for several local colleges where he spent many years working with staff members as well as the executive leadership in building technical education programs.

John served as vice-president of the advisory board for a local college where his duties entail working with city, county, and state leadership and government officials to help build support and funding for the Northwest Wyoming Community College District in Wyoming. He has also sat on an advisory board for a local high school and was very passionate about his work there, which included student engagement, or how to keep students in school.

John retired from his position as Director of Training from a large mining organization in March of 2012 after spending 34 years there. While there, he helped develop and conduct training for all levels within the organization. This included working closely with various global training providers to develop, and then conduct, training for all 14,000 employees within the organization.

In 2010, John entered into an agreement with a private firm and co-authored a succession-planning program which is currently being taught throughout the world. He was also jointly responsible for the recruitment and hiring process for the company's Wyoming mining operations and worked closely with the Federal Government to set up and manage apprenticeship programs throughout the organization. John was often called upon to help with conflict resolution both internally and externally.

John joined Peregrine Leadership Institute and Peregrine Academic Services as Executive Director shortly after his retirement from the mining industry. John oversees the daily business functions of Peregrine Leadership Institute and conducts executive leadership programs to various clients.

Deborah K. Robbins, MPA

Deborah Robbins has an extensive background in Human Resources, leadership development, HR systems, and strategic planning. Her undergraduate degree is in Personnel Management and Industrial Relations and she holds a Master's degree in Public Administration. Throughout her years of public service in local government, her focus was on leadership development, general human resource practices, and project management.

Ms. Robbins also has extensive experience in the private sector with general human resources, recruiting, and continuous improvement processes. She is an adjunct faculty member for the University of Mary in Bismarck, ND, teaching undergraduate and graduate level Human Resources and Diversity courses. Ms. Robbins holds the certification of Senior Professional in Human Resources from the Society of Human Resources in the U.S.

In 2010 Ms. Robbins joined Peregrine Leadership Institute, focusing on instructional design, human resource consulting, executive leadership development, and coaching new supervisors. She currently resides in Mudgee, New South Wales, Australia.

Index of Key Topics

Index of Key Lists